Strengthening Physical Science Skills for Middle & Upper Grades

By
MYRL SHIREMAN

COPYRIGHT © 2008 Mark Twain Media, Inc.

ISBN: 978-1-58037-453-8

Printing No. CD-404094

Mark Twain Media, Inc., Publishers
Distributed by Carson-Dellosa Publishing Company, Inc.

Table of Contents

Supplemental CD-ROM

> **Introduction**
>
> **Activities corresponding to each chapter in each of the following categories:**
>
>> **Science Reading Exercises (printable)**
>>
>> **Printable Physical Science Worksheets**
>>
>> **Interactive Exercises**
>>
>>> **Classroom Version**
>>>
>>> **E-mail Version**

Introduction

When compared to international students, students in the United States do not score well on physical science aptitude tests. This is particularly true as students progress into the middle school years and beyond. This book is written to encourage students at the middle school level and beyond to develop an interest and the confidence to succeed in physical science and more rigorous science courses.

The activities in the book are developed around major physical science concepts. Science vocabulary is important to understanding science subjects. Activities are developed to help students become familiar with the vocabulary critical to understanding the science content. The science content and activities in *Strengthening Physical Science Skills for the Middle and Upper Grades* have been developed to meet many of the recommendations from the National Science Education Standards. Mathematics activities have been included: the National Science Education Standards recommend that mathematics instruction should be a part of science content. A review of physical science standards from many states, including California, Minnesota, and Georgia, has been incorporated into the physical science exercises in *Strengthening Physical Science Skills for the Middle and Upper Grades*.

The accompanying CD-ROM contains interactive exercises that focus on math skills related to the physical science concepts. Students enter their answers in the exercises on the screen. The program then scores the exercise and prints a hard copy. One version of the interactive exercises can be completed in the classroom. A separate version of the interactive exercises can be e-mailed to the student to be completed at home. Printable science worksheets are also included on the CD-ROM. These worksheets focus on the physical science concepts and technical vocabulary. These worksheets are meant to be printed out by instructors or parents for students to complete on the hard copy. Answer keys are provided.

Students in the middle grades and beyond often experience difficulty in reading scientific content because of the many special vocabulary words, as well as an increase in the number of words with three or more syllables. These words significantly increase the content reading level. On the accompanying CD-ROM reading exercises, words from each chapter with three or more syllables are identified. The printable CD-ROM exercises will help students read these multisyllabic words and understand their meanings. Learning these words and their meanings raises reading comprehension levels for all students. These multisyllabic words are words students will encounter in science courses in later grades. The CD-ROM reading exercises are developed to be printed out and used as chapter previews prior to instruction or as meaningful homework assignments that parents, tutors, teacher aides, and others can teach effectively.

State and National Science Standards

State Standards: Grades 6, 7, & 8: Minnesota

The student will:

- Know that there are more than 100 unique elements.
- Use evidence to explain that matter is made up of atoms, or molecules.
- Know that the mass of a substance remains constant.
- Distinguish between volume, mass, and density.
- Know that atoms are the smallest unit of an element that maintains the characteristics of the element.
- Demonstrate that visible light from the sun or reflected objects may be made of a mixture of many different colors of light.
- Describe waves in terms of speed, frequency, and wavelength.
- Recognize that vibrations, such as sound and earthquakes, move in waves and that waves move at different speeds in different materials.
- Use a frame of reference to describe the position, speed, and acceleration of an object.
- Measure and graph the positions and speed of an object.
- Recognize that unbalanced forces acting on an object change the speed and/or direction.
- Know that there are positive and negative charges and that like charges repel one another and opposite charges attract.

State Standards: Grade 7: California

Students know:

- That visible light is a small band within a very broad electromagnetic spectrum.
- That for an object to be seen, light transmitted by or scattered from it must be detected by the eye.
- Light travels in straight lines if the medium it travels through does not change.
- That white light is a mixture of many wavelengths (colors) and that the retinal cells react differently to different wavelengths.
- Light can be reflected, refracted, transmitted, and absorbed by matter.
- That the angle of reflection is equal to the angle of incidence.

State Standards: Grade 8: California
Students know:
- Velocity is a change in position.
- Unbalanced forces cause a change in velocity.
- Direction and magnitude.
- The more mass, the greater the force to change velocity.
- Each of the 100-plus elements have distinct properties and a distinct atomic structure.
- All forms of matter are composed of one or more elements.
- Matter is composed of protons, electrons, and neutrons.
- The states of matter are solid, liquid, and gas.
- How to use the periodic table to identify elements and compounds.
- Density has mass per volume.
- How to calculate density of substances; students know how to predict whether an object will float or sink.

State Standards: Grade 5 Mathematics: Georgia
- Measurement including circumference, area, weight/mass, gram, pound, kilogram

State Standards: Georgia
Students will:
- Investigate the properties of waves.
- Determine the relationship between forces, mass, and motion.
- Explore the nature of matter, its classifications, and its system of naming matter.
- Investigate the arrangement of the Periodic Table.
- Investigate the current understanding of the atom.

State Standards: Grade 8: Wisconsin
- Properties and changes of properties in matter

State Standards: Physical Science Standards: Tennessee
- Standard Number 1.0: Force and Motion
- Standard Number 2.0: Structure and Properties of Matter
- Standard Number 4.0: Energy

State Standards: South Carolina
- A. Motions and Forces
- C. Interaction of Energy and Matter

National Standards: Grades 5–8
Students should develop an understanding of:
- Properties and changes in properties in matter.
- Motions and forces.
- Transfer of energy.

Name: _____ Date: _____

Chapter I: Atoms, Molecules, and Compounds

Atoms

All objects are made of atoms. An **atom** is the smallest piece of matter that still has all the properties of an object. Each atom has protons, electrons, and neutrons. The Bohr model is often used to show the structure of atoms. In this model, the atom may be thought of like our solar system. Look at the diagram at the right. The sun (a) is the center of our solar system. The planets (b) revolve around the sun. Similarly, the nucleus (a) is the center of an atom. Protons (b) and neutrons (c) are in the nucleus. The electrons (d) are in orbit around the nucleus, much like the planets orbit around the sun.

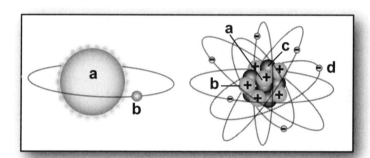

Protons, Neutrons, and Electrons

Protons and neutrons are in the nucleus of the atom. The **protons** have a positive charge. The **neutrons** are neutral, which means that they do not have a charge. The **electrons** have a negative charge. They are in shells around the nucleus. In most atoms, the number of protons and electrons are equal. However, an atom may lose or gain electrons. If the atom has more protons, the atom has a positive charge. If an atom has more electrons than protons, then the atom has a negative charge.

Circle the correct word(s) or write in the answers to complete the following sentences.

1. The smallest particle of an element is the (atom / proton / electron).

2. The parts of an atom are the _____, _____, and _____.

3. The (protons / electrons) have a positive charge.

4. The (protons / electrons) have a negative charge.

5. The (protons / electrons / neutrons) have no charge.

6. In most atoms, the number of protons and electrons are (equal / unequal).

7. An atom may lose (protons / electrons).

8. If an atom has more protons than electrons, the atom has a (positive / negative) charge.

9. If an atom has more electrons than protons, then the atom has a (positive / negative) charge.

Name: _____   Date: _____

Elements

   Elements are pure substances. Each element is made up of only one type of atom. Each atom in a given element has the same number of protons. If you change the number of protons in an elemental atom, then you have a different element. There are over 113 different elements. The Periodic Table lists all of the known elements according to how many protons are in each atom.

Use the Periodic Table and write the number of protons on the blank. *Hint: The number of protons equals the atomic number.*

1. Oxygen (O)   _____   2. Gold (Au)   _____

3. Iron (Fe)   _____   4. Helium (He)   _____

5. Hydrogen (H) _____

Molecules

   Molecules form when two or more atoms join together. The molecule may be small, or it may be large. Molecules may be made up of atoms from the same element, or they may be made of atoms from different elements.

Each of the small circles in A, B, and C below is an atom. The atoms have joined to form molecules. On each blank, write the letter SE if the molecule is made of atoms from the same element. Write the letters DE if the molecule is made up of atoms of different elements.

| ○ Oxygen atom |
| ● Hydrogen atom |

A.   B.   C.

_____   _____   _____

Complete the following sentences using the terms oxygen or hydrogen.

1. The molecules labeled ***SE*** are made of _____ atoms.

2. A molecule labeled ***DE*** is made of _____ and _____ atoms.

Name: _____ Date: _____

Compounds

When molecules made from atoms of different elements join together, a **compound** is formed. Compounds are molecules. However, a molecule is not a compound if it is made of a single element. Compounds are the atoms joined from more than one element. Water is a compound. One oxygen atom and two hydrogen atoms make a water molecule. You cannot see the separate parts of a compound. However, just as the number of protons determines the element, the number of atoms in a compound determine the compound. A water compound is two hydrogen atoms and one oxygen atom. If the molecule was made of two hydrogen atoms and two oxygen atoms, the compound would no longer be water, but hydrogen peroxide!

*For each set of atoms below, determine if the atoms are a compound or an element. Write the letter **C** on the blank if the atoms form a compound. Place the letter **E** on the blank if the atoms form an element.*

1. _____
2. _____
3. _____
4. _____
5. _____

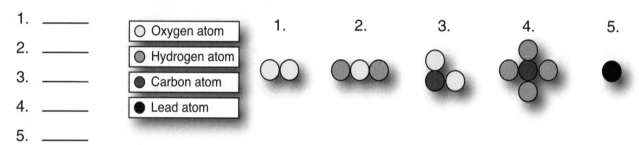

Mixtures

Mixtures consist of two or more substances that do not chemically combine with each other. The substances in mixtures keep their separate identities and properties, even if they display some special properties while they are in the mixture. Think of a bean salad as a mixture. Different kinds of beans are mixed together, but they can still be identified as separate beans. The substances that make up a mixture can often be separated. There may be many elements or compounds in a mixture, but all of them can be separated back out to the individual components by ordinary physical methods.

Place a plus sign (+) on the blank if the substance is a mixture, and a minus sign (–) if it is a compound.

_____ 1. A potato and bean salad

_____ 2. Banana, peach, and orange fruit salad

_____ 3. Water

_____ 4. Soda with ice cubes

_____ 5. Birdseed with many kinds of seeds

_____ 6. Salt water

_____ 7. Salt

_____ 8. Rust

Name: _____ Date: _____

 # Chapter II: Chemistry

The Periodic Table

Symbols

There are over 113 elements found on Earth. For example, iron is an element. The only atoms in a pound of iron are iron atoms. Each element has unique characteristics. The **Periodic Table** is a way of organizing elements to make them easy to understand. The Periodic Table gives important data about each element. The first thing you will notice about the Periodic Table is that each element has its own symbol. The chemical symbol for all elements includes a capital letter. The symbol for oxygen is shown by the symbol O. Some elements have a capital letter and one or two small letters. Two elements found on the Periodic Table are iron and copper. The symbol for iron is Fe. The symbol for copper is Cu.

The Periodic Table of the Elements

1																	18

1	Alkali Metals		
2	Alkaline Earth Metals		
3 – 12	Transition Metals		
13–16	BCNO Groups		
17	Halogens		
18	Noble Gases		

Liquid - Br, Hg   **Gas** - H, He, N, O, F, Ne, Cl, Ar, Kr, Xe, Rn   **Solid** - All Others

Using the Periodic Table, find the symbols for each of the following elements.

1. Gold _____
2. Helium _____
3. Neon _____
4. Aluminum _____
5. Radium _____
6. Cesium _____
7. Chlorine _____
8. Sulfur _____

Name: _____ Date: _____

Atomic Number

In addition to a symbol, each of the 113 elements has an atomic number on the Periodic Table. The **atomic number** is the same as the number of protons in an atom of the element. Atoms do not lose protons. They always have the same number of protons. If an element's atom were to lose a proton, it would then be a different element.

Use the Periodic Table to find the symbol and atomic number for each element. Write the symbols and atomic numbers on the blanks by the element.

Element	Symbol	Atomic Number
1. Aluminum	_____	_____
2. Oxygen	_____	_____
3. Iron	_____	_____
4. Lead	_____	_____
5. Mercury	_____	_____
6. Sodium	_____	_____
7. Copper	_____	_____
8. Gold	_____	_____
9. Helium	_____	_____
10. Radium	_____	_____
11. Radon	_____	_____
12. Carbon	_____	_____
13. Nickel	_____	_____
14. Hydrogen	_____	_____
15. Potassium	_____	_____
16. Neon	_____	_____
17. Nitrogen	_____	_____
18. Zinc	_____	_____
19. Cobalt	_____	_____
20. Phosphorus	_____	_____
21. Calcium	_____	_____

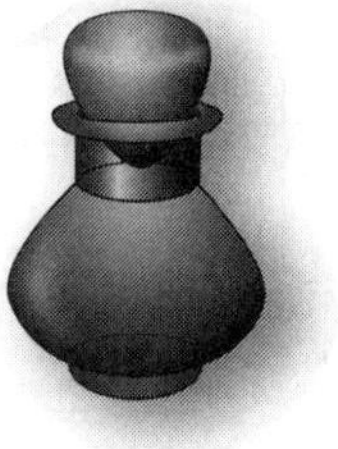

Name: _____ Date: _____

Chemical Formulas

As you already learned, when elements combine, the resulting substance is a compound. **Chemical formulas** are a kind of shorthand used to show the amounts of different elements in a compound. Let's look at the compound water. Water is made up of two hydrogen atoms and one oxygen atom. The chemical formula for water is H_2O. The $_2$ shows that there are two hydrogen atoms. Because it has no number, the O tells us there is only one oxygen atom in the formula.

Use the Periodic Table to complete the blanks.

Compound Formula	Number of Elements in Compound	Element Names
1. H_2O	_____	_____
2. CO_2	_____	_____
3. $PbSO_3$	_____	_____
4. Na_2O_3	_____	_____

Fill in the blanks to complete the following sentences.

5. In the formula H_2O there are 2 atoms of _____ and 1 atom of

   _____.

6. In the formula CO_2 there is 1 atom of _____ and 2 atoms of

   _____.

7. In the formula $PbSO_3$ there is 1 atom of _____, 1 atom of

   _____, and 3 atoms of _____.

8. In the formula Na_2O_3 there are 2 atoms of _____ and 3 atoms of

   _____.

Review

Match the items with the correct definition.

_____ 1. Protons

_____ 2. Compound

_____ 3. Electrons

_____ 4. Neutrons

_____ 5. Mixture

_____ 6. Atom

A. Found in the shells of an atom, circling the nucleus

B. Found in the atom nucleus with the protons

C. Can be separated back out into its individual substances with ordinary physical methods

D. The number of these is the atomic number.

E. Atoms of more than one element bond together to form a new substance.

F. The smallest particle into which an element can be divided without changing its chemical and physical properties

Name: _____ Date: _____

Chapter III: States of Matter

Matter

To understand science, it is important to understand matter. All objects are made of matter. There are three states of matter. The three states of matter are solids, liquids, and gases. Atoms are found in all solids, liquids, and gases. However, the movement of atoms in solids, liquids, and gases is not the same. Think of a glass of water that has accidentally been knocked over. The glass is a solid. In **solids**, the atoms are not free to move, so the glass does not change shape. The water is a liquid. In **liquids**, the atoms can move more freely than in a solid. The water had the same shape as the glass, but after it was spilled, it took the shape of the tabletop. However, there is still the same amount of water. Eventually, if no one wipes up the spill, the liquid will change into a gas, water vapor. In **gases**, the atoms have the greatest freedom of movement. The atoms of gas will expand and fill the container holding them. The water vapor will expand to fill the room.

Complete the Cloze using the words in bold. Words may be used more than once.

| gases | atoms | liquids | solids |

There are three states of matter. The three states of matter are (1) _____,

liquids, and gases. Atoms are found in all solids, (2) _____, and (3) _____.

However, the movement of atoms in solids, liquids, and gases is not the same. Think of a

glass of water that has accidentally been knocked over. The glass is a solid. In solids, the

(4) _____ are not free to move, so the glass does not change shape. The water is

a liquid. In (5) _____, the atoms can move more freely than in a (6) _____.

The water had the same shape as the glass, but after it was spilled, it took the shape of the

tabletop. However, there is still the same amount of water. Eventually, if no one wipes up the

spill, the liquid will change into a gas, water vapor. In (7) _____, the atoms have

the greatest freedom of movement. The atoms of gas will expand and fill the container

holding them. The water vapor will expand to fill the room.

Name: _____   Date: _____

Volume

All forms of matter have volume. **Volume** is a measurement of how much space an object takes up. Matter in a solid state has a specific volume and shape. The volume and shape do not change. Matter in a liquid state has a specific volume, but not a specific shape. Matter in a liquid state maintains the same volume, but takes the shape of the container that holds it. Matter in a gas state has volume, but the volume of a gas depends on the size of the container. Gases do not have shape. The atoms are free to move around. The atoms expand to fill the container that holds them. Pressure can reduce the volume of gases to fit a container.

Each of the solid objects below takes up space, and each object has volume.

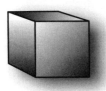 

The liquid below has a specific volume, but it takes the shape of the container that holds it.

Shade the containers according to the information below.

Containers *A*, *B*, *C*, and *D* are all the same height. Container *A* holds 1 gallon of liquid. Container *B* will hold 5 gallons of liquid, Container *C* will hold 2 gallons, and Container *D* will hold 8 gallons. Container *A* is filled with liquid. The liquid from *A* is poured into *B*, *C*, and *D*. Estimate and shade in the level of the liquid in *B*, *C*, and *D*.

A.   B.   C.   D.

Name: _____ Date: _____

Density

      Density is how closely the atoms of an object are packed. Different substances have different densities. Frequently, solids are more dense than liquids or gases. Liquids are often more dense than gases. Gases usually are the least dense. However, this is not always true. Let's look at water in its three states. Solid water is ice, and gaseous water is water vapor. Water vapor is less dense than liquid water, so it rises up in the air. However, ice is also less dense than liquid water, so it floats on the top of liquid water. A rock is more dense than liquid water, so it sinks. Wood is less dense than water, so it floats. Helium, a gas, has less density than oxygen or nitrogen, so balloons filled with helium float, while balloons you blow up yourself sink to the ground.

Circle the correct word(s) to complete the following sentences.

1. All gases have (similar / different) densities.

2. All liquids have (similar / different) densities.

3. All solids have (similar / different) densities.

4. Water in the liquid state is (more / less) dense than water in the gas state.

5. Water in the liquid state is (more / less) dense than water in the solid state.

6. There are equal volumes of water and lead. The density of atoms in water is (more / less) than the density of atoms in lead.

7. Density is determined by (weight / atoms).

Boyle's Law for Gas

      Boyle's law states that if pressure and temperature remain constant and unchanged, the volume of a gas remains unchanged. However, Boyle's law states that if pressure on a gas increases, the volume of the gas decreases. Inversely, if pressure on a gas decreases, the volume of that gas increases. What does that mean? Well, imagine you blow up a balloon in a 65° room. The gas in the balloon fills the volume of the balloon shape. If you then put the balloon in the refrigerator for an hour, the balloon would shrink. Gas did not leak out of the balloon: instead, the cooler temperature caused the volume of the air to decrease. Now put the balloon in a room that is 95° for an hour. The balloon will have expanded past its original size; perhaps it even burst. There was not more air in the balloon, but the warmer temperatures caused the atoms in the gas to expand.

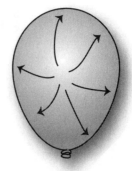

Name: _____   Date: _____

Circle the correct answers based on the information given below.

Container *A* has a volume of one gallon. It has been filled with atoms in a gas form. Pressure is applied to the top of Container *A*, reducing its volume. The amount of atoms has not changed. Containers *B*, *C*, and *D* below show the approximate volume of the containers as pressure increases.

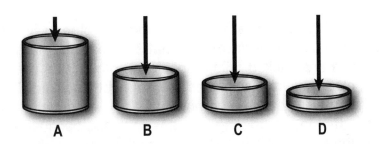

1. The pressure has been increased on Container *A* until it is the same as Container *B*. The

   volume in *B* is about _____ that of Container *A*.

   a) $\frac{1}{2}$ b) $\frac{1}{3}$

   c) $\frac{1}{4}$ d) $\frac{1}{5}$

2. The pressure has been increased on Container *B* until it is the same as Container *C*. The

   volume in *C* is about _____ that of Container *A*.

   a) $\frac{1}{2}$ b) $\frac{1}{3}$

   c) $\frac{1}{4}$ d) $\frac{1}{5}$

3. The pressure has been increased on Container *C* until it is the same as Container *D*. The

   volume in *D* is about _____ that of Container *A*.

   a) $\frac{1}{2}$ b) $\frac{1}{3}$

   c) $\frac{1}{4}$ d) $\frac{1}{5}$

4. In Containers *A*, *B*, *C*, and *D*, as the pressure increases, the number of atoms that make

   up the gas is (unchanged / changed).

5. As the pressure increases, the volume of the gas in Containers *A*, *B*, *C*, and *D* (increases /

   decreases).

Name: _____ Date: _____

Chapter IV: Mass, Weight, Gravity, and Density

Matter, Mass, and Weight

As we have learned, all objects are made of atoms. Another way to talk about the atoms that make up objects is to use the term *matter*. **Matter** is basically large groups of atoms. In some objects, the atoms are packed tightly near each other. This makes the matter of the object very dense. In other objects, the atoms are not tightly packed. This makes the matter of the object less dense. Say you have a bowling ball and a foam ball the same size. Both are made of matter. The matter in the bowling ball is very dense because the atoms are closely packed. The matter in the foam ball is not as dense as the bowling ball because the atoms are more spaced out.

The way to talk about an object having more matter is to talk about its **mass**. Because more atoms are packed in the same space, the bowling ball has more mass. The foam ball has less mass because it has fewer atoms packed into the same space. Mass is the amount of physical matter in an object. Mass does not change with the location of the object.

Because the bowling ball has more mass that the foam ball, it also weighs more. You can easily kick a foam ball a great distance because it is lightweight. However, if you tried to kick a bowling ball, you might break your foot! The **weight** of an object is a measurement of the force of gravity pulling the object toward the Earth's center. While the matter and mass of a bowling ball will not change, the weight might. If you were to go bowling at the bottom of the ocean, the bowling ball would be much heavier because you are closer to the center of the earth. If you were to go bowling in a space shuttle that is orbiting the earth, the bowling ball would be much lighter because you are much farther from the center of the earth. While the amount of matter and the mass of the bowling ball doesn't change, the weight does.

Place a T on the blank if the statement is true. Place an F on the blank if the statement is false.

_____ 1. Mass and weight are the same thing.

_____ 2. The mass of an object is greater on Earth's surface than the mass of the object 1,000 feet away from Earth's surface.

_____ 3. A dense object has the atoms packed very closely together.

_____ 4. A bowling ball is more dense than a foam ball that is the same size.

_____ 5. Gravity affects weight but does not affect mass.

_____ 6. A brick taken to the moon would have the same weight as on Earth.

_____ 7. The mass of an object depends on the amount of matter in the object.

_____ 8. The weight of an object depends on gravity.

_____ 9. The mass of a brick would be less 1,000 feet away from Earth's surface than on Earth's surface.

_____ 10. The weight of a brick is a measure of the pull of gravity.

Name: _____ Date: _____

Mass Measurement

How do you measure mass? There are several different ways to measure mass. Most people in the United States measure mass using the **English, or standard, system**. This system uses ounces (oz.) and pounds (lbs.) to measure mass. There are 16 ounces in a pound. We go to the store and buy a pound of apples to make a pie. However, while widely used, the standard system is not the most accurate. You may have noticed when you buy a bag of chips at the store that its weight will first be listed in ounces or pounds, but that there is a second number in parentheses after it. For instance, a snack bag of chips may say 2 oz. (56.7 g). The g stands for grams. Grams are units of measurement used in the **metric system**. Other units of metric measurement include milligrams (mg = 1/1,000 of a gram) and kilograms (kg = 1,000 grams). The metric system can more accurately measure objects and is therefore more commonly used in science.

To convert between the standard system and the metric system, it is helpful to keep a few numbers in mind:

1,000 g = 1 kilogram   1 kilogram = 2.2 pounds
454 g = 1 pound   1 pound = 0.454 kilograms

Complete the following chart.

	Grams	=	Kilograms	=	Pounds
1.	500	=	_____	=	_____
2.	2,000	=	_____	=	_____
3.	4,000	=	_____	=	_____
4.	4,500	=	_____	=	_____
5.	_____	=	5	=	_____
6.	_____	=	7	=	_____
7.	_____	=	_____	=	22
8.	_____	=	1.5	=	_____
9.	100	=	_____	=	_____
10.	_____	=	0.25	=	_____

Name: _____ Date: _____

Gravity and Weight

Gravity

What is gravity? **Gravity** is a constant force exerted by objects that have mass. An object that has mass has gravity. It may seem strange, but you, your chair, this book, and your pencil all have gravity, because they all have mass. All objects with mass are pulling on all other objects. However, your pencil does not have a great deal of mass, so it has a tiny amount of gravity, so small that you cannot feel it. In fact, the only thing that has enough mass to produce enough gravity for you to feel is Earth. Have you ever fallen while riding your bike or roller blading? Gravity pulled you to the ground. The mass of the earth was so great that it tried to pull you to the center of the earth. Gravity is the reason you don't just float out of your chair right now. Gravity holds the earth in orbit as it travels around the sun. It is the force that holds the moon in orbit around the earth.

When one steps on a scale, the scale shows the pull of gravity on the person being weighed. Gravity is a force that pulls things toward the center of the Earth. The force of gravity pulls on the mass of the person being weighed. The force is shown as a weight reading on the scale. Those who have more mass weigh more.

Weight on Earth

Weight is the pull of gravity. The scale shows the pull of gravity on the mass of our body. The pull of gravity on our body mass is toward the center of the Earth. Weight shows on the scale because the pull of gravity is pulling against the scale toward the center of the Earth. The scale is held firm on the floor. Weight is unlike mass. Weight changes if the gravity changes. Mass does not change. However, the pull of gravity is constant on the surface of the earth, so we use the same units of measurement, pounds and kilograms, to measure mass and weight.

1,000 milligrams = 1 gram	28.35 grams = 1 ounce	1 gram = 0.003527 ounce
1,000 grams = 1 kilogram	1 kilogram = 2.205 pounds	454 g = 1 pound

Solve the following problems.

1. A friend tells you that he weighs 40 kilograms. The friend's weight in pounds is

    a) 22.   b) 80.   c) 66.   d) 88.2.

2. A box is weighed. The scale shows 11 pounds. The box's weight in kilograms is

    a) 2.   b) 5.   c) 7.   d) 9.

3. A small package weighs 10 ounces. The package's weight in grams is

    a) 83.5.   b) 183.5.   c) 283.5.   d) 383.5.

4. A box of candy shows the weight as 500 grams. The weight of the candy in kilograms is

    a) $\frac{1}{4}$ b) $\frac{1}{5}$ c) $\frac{1}{3}$ d) $\frac{1}{2}$ kilogram.

5. A package of hamburger weighs 227 grams. The meat's weight in pounds is

    a) $\frac{1}{4}$ b) $\frac{1}{2}$ c) $\frac{1}{3}$ d) $\frac{1}{8}$ pound.

Name: _____ Date: _____

Place the letter _T_ on the blank if the statement is true. Place the letter _F_ on the blank if the statement is false.

_____ 6. Weight is the pull of gravity on an object.

_____ 7. The pull of gravity is toward the center of the earth.

_____ 8. It takes 1,000 milligrams to equal one gram.

_____ 9. An object that weighs 1 kilogram weighs less than 1 pound.

_____ 10. To change 10 kilograms to pounds, you must multiply 10 • 2.205.

_____ 11. One thousand grams equals one pound.

_____ 12. One thousand grams equals one kilogram.

Weight and Gravity on Earth and the Moon

We know that weight is a measure of the force of gravity of one object with mass pulling on the mass of another object. For us, that means that gravity is pulling all objects on Earth to the center of the earth. But did you know that the force of gravity is stronger the closer two objects are together? It's true! An object on Earth's surface weighs more than the same object high above the earth's surface. You would actually weigh less in Denver, Colorado, than you would in New Orleans, Louisiana, because New Orleans is about 1 mile closer to the center of the earth than Denver. (After all, Denver is the Mile-High City.) The differences would be small—no more than a milligram, but still, the pull of gravity is a bit stronger in New Orleans. As the object gets farther from the center of the earth, the force pulling on the object is less.

An object on the moon weighs less than the same object on Earth, because the moon has less mass than the earth. Objects are pulled toward the center of the moon with less force of gravity than on Earth. The weight of an object on Earth is greater than the weight of the object on the moon. The greater weight is because the mass of the earth is greater. The earth's mass is approximately six times that of the moon. Objects on Earth weigh about six times more than they would on the moon. Because weight depends on how far an object is from the center of the planet, an object that is not near any planet does not have any weight. There is no planet to pull on the object. The object floats and does not fall.

Solve these problems. Circle the letter of the correct answer for each.

1. An object that weighs 1 kilogram on the moon would weigh   a) 2   b) 3   c) 6   d) 8 kilograms on Earth.

2. An object that weighs 1 kilogram on the moon would weigh   a) 3.205   b) 2.205 c) 4.205   d) 5.205   pounds on the moon.

3. An object that weighs 6 kilograms on Earth would weigh   a) 2.205   b) 4.41 c) 11.02   d) 17.64   pounds on the moon.

4. An object on Earth weighs 60 pounds. The object is taken to the moon, where it will weigh one-sixth as much. The weight of the object on the moon will be

   a) 10   b) 20   c) 40   d) 60   pounds.

Name: _____ Date: _____

Weight in Newtons

Weight may be measured in a unit of force called a **newton**. A standard pound is equivalent to 4.45 newtons. To change pounds to newtons, take the weight in pounds times 4.45. If an object weighs 100 pounds, it weighs 445 newtons (100 • 4.45 = 445). To change 445 newtons back to pounds, you must divide. You divide 445 by 4.45. (445 ÷ 4.45 = 100 pounds)

Converting Pounds to Newtons

Change the pounds to newtons.

	Pounds		Newtons
1.	1	=	4.5
2.	10	=	_____
3.	100	=	_____
4.	150	=	_____
5.	200	=	_____

Converting Newtons to Pounds

Change the newtons to pounds.

	Newtons		Pounds
6.	10	=	2.25
7.	133.5	=	_____
8.	778.75	=	_____
9.	356	=	_____
10.	2,225	=	_____

Converting Kilograms to Newtons

One kilogram is pulled toward the center of Earth with a force of 9.8 newtons. To change kilograms to newtons, multiply kilograms times 9.8.

Change the kilograms to newtons.

	Kilograms		Newtons
11.	1	=	9.8
12.	10	=	_____
13.	100	=	_____
14.	500	=	_____
15.	1,000	=	_____

Converting Newtons to Kilograms

To change newtons to kilograms, you must divide newtons by 9.8.

Change the newtons to kilograms.

	Newtons		Kilograms
16.	9.8	=	_____
17.	98	=	_____
18.	989	=	_____
19.	9,898	=	_____
20.	989,898	=	_____

Name: _____ Date: _____

Newton's Law of Gravity

How can we figure the force of gravity? Most everyone has heard the story of Isaac Newton and the apple. Newton was resting under a tree when an apple hit him in the head, and, inspired by that event, he calculated the **Law of Gravity**. The law states that one must know the masses of the objects and distance the objects are apart to determine what the force of gravity is. Newton's law states that "the greater the mass of the objects, the more they attract." The law also says that "the farther objects are from each other, the less they attract." The attraction decreases as a square of the distance between the objects. This is known as the **Inverse Square Rule**. This rule tells us that as the distance between the objects increases, the objects attract less and less. Newton's formula for finding the force of gravity is:

$$Fg = G \bullet Mass_1 \bullet Mass_2 / r^2$$

Fg = force of gravity. $Mass_1$ is the mass of the first object. $Mass_2$ is the mass of the second object. $Mass_1$ is multiplied by $Mass_2$, and the result is divided by r^2, which is the radius of the distance between the center of $Mass_1$ and the center of $Mass_2$. G is the universal gravitational constant.

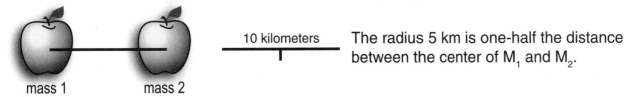

10 kilometers   The radius 5 km is one-half the distance between the center of M₁ and M₂.

mass 1   mass 2

For our purposes, we do not need to figure G, so use the formula $Fg = M_1 \bullet M_2 / r^2$

> **Example A:** The mass of $Mass_1$ is 50 kilograms. The mass of $Mass_2$ is 40 kilograms. The distance between the center of $Mass_1$ and the center of $Mass_2$ is 10 kilometers. The radius is one-half the 10 kilometers, so the radius is 5 kilometers.
>
> So our equation looks like this:
> $Fg = M_1 \bullet M_2 / r^2 \longrightarrow Fg = (50 \bullet 40)/(5^2) \longrightarrow Fg = 2{,}000/25 \longrightarrow Fg = 80$

As the distance between the two objects increases, the force of gravity between the two objects decreases. This is an **inverse relationship**. An increase in one brings a decrease in the other.

20 kilometers   The radius 10 km is $\frac{1}{2}$ the distance between the center of M₁ and M₂.

mass 1   mass 2

> **Example B:** The mass of $Mass_1$ is 50 kilograms. The mass of $Mass_2$ is 40 kilograms. The distance between $Mass_1$ and $Mass_2$ is 20 kilometers. The radius is one-half the 20 kilometers, so the radius is 10 kilometers.

Name: _____ Date: _____

Force of gravity: $Fg = M_1 \cdot M_2 / r^2$ $Fg = (50 \cdot 40)/(10^2)$ $Fg = 2,000/100$ $Fg = 20$

The distance between $Mass_1$ and $Mass_2$ is two times greater in B. The mass of both A and B did not change as the distance between $Mass_1$ and $Mass_2$ increased. But the force of gravity decreased by one-fourth ($20/80 = 1/4$) in B. This is an inverse square relationship. The distance doubled, while the force of gravity decreased by the inverse of the square of the amount the distance increased.

Solve the following.

For each of the problems that follow, the mass of $Mass_1$ and $Mass_2$ will be the same. Only the distance between $Mass_1$ and $Mass_2$ will change. Complete the blanks for $Fg = M_1 \cdot M_2 / r^2$ and find Fg.

$Mass_1 = 1,000$ kg   **$Mass_2 = 40$ kg**

1. The distance between $Mass_1$ and $Mass_2$ is 60 kilometers. The radius is $\frac{1}{2}$ the

    60 kilometers.

    $Fg = M_1 \cdot M_2 / r^2$ $Fg = ($_____ • _____$) /$ _____

    $Fg = 40,000 / 900$ $Fg = $ _____

2. The distance between $Mass_1$ and $Mass_2$ is 120 kilometers. The radius is $\frac{1}{2}$ the

    120 kilometers.

    $Fg = M_1 \cdot M_2 / r^2$ $Fg = ($_____ • _____$) /$ _____

    $Fg = 40,000 / 3,600$ $Fg = $ _____

3. The distance between M_1 and M_2 (increased / decreased) and the force of gravity

    (increased / decreased).

4. The distance between $Mass_1$ and $Mass_2$ is 180 kilometers. The radius is $\frac{1}{2}$ the

    180 kilometers.

    $Fg = M_1 \cdot M_2 / r^2$ $Fg = ($_____ • _____$) /$ _____

    $Fg = 40,000 / 8,100$ $Fg = $ _____

Name: _____ Date: _____

Newtons and Force

In our equation $Fg = M_1 \cdot M_2 / r^2 \longrightarrow Fg = (50 \cdot 40)/(5^2) \longrightarrow Fg = 2,000/25 \longrightarrow Fg = 80$, you may be wondering, 80 *what?* The answer is another unit of measurement. This unit is called a ***newton***. The newton is a unit of force. The symbol for newtons is (N). We have already converted pounds and kilograms to newtons and newtons to pounds and kilograms.

So let's discuss how you would actually use newtons to figure gravity. What happened when the apple fell out of the tree? The apple fell with a certain velocity. **Velocity** is measured in distance over time, which is meters over seconds, or $v = m/sec$. You may be more familiar with miles per hour, or *mph*, from riding in a car. Both mph and m/sec measure the same thing, velocity, but they use different units of measurement to do it.

Back to the apple. When the apple first fell, it had no velocity—it wasn't moving. By the time it hit Newton in the head, it was going much faster. The difference between its starting speed of zero and its final speed is the **acceleration.** Acceleration is a unit of velocity over the unit of time. If your car goes from 0 to 60 in 5 seconds, then the formula would be 60 mph/ 5. In science, this formula is written as $a = (m/sec)/sec$. The final piece to the puzzle is force. **Force = mass • acceleration** or $F = m \cdot a$. A newton is the force needed to accelerate an object with a mass of one kilogram at a rate of one meter per second squared, or $(kg \cdot m)/sec^2$. When we use N for newton, we are using shorthand for $(kg \cdot m)/sec^2$. One newton is about 9.81 kilograms.

In the problems below, complete the blanks $F = (\underline{\hspace{1cm}}$ kg • $\underline{\hspace{1cm}}$ m)/s² to find the force in newtons.

Complete the blanks to find the force in newtons.

1. An object has a mass of 1 kilogram. How many newtons will it take to accelerate the object 1 meter in 1 second? $F = (\underline{\hspace{1cm}}$ kg • $\underline{\hspace{1cm}}$ m)/ $\underline{\hspace{1cm}}$ s² $F = \underline{\hspace{1cm}}$ N

2. An object has a mass of 3 kilograms. How many newtons will it take to accelerate the object 1 meter in 1 second? $F = (\underline{\hspace{1cm}}$ kg • $\underline{\hspace{1cm}}$ m)/ $\underline{\hspace{1cm}}$ s² $F = \underline{\hspace{1cm}}$

3. An object has a mass of 5 kilograms. How many newtons will it take to accelerate the object 1 meter in 1 second? $F = (\underline{\hspace{1cm}}$ kg • $\underline{\hspace{1cm}}$ m)/ $\underline{\hspace{1cm}}$ s² $F = \underline{\hspace{1cm}}$

4. An object has a mass of 10 kilograms. How many newtons will it take to accelerate the object 1 meter in 1 second? $F = (\underline{\hspace{1cm}}$ kg • $\underline{\hspace{1cm}}$ m)/ $\underline{\hspace{1cm}}$ s² $F = \underline{\hspace{1cm}}$

5. An object has a mass of 100 kilograms. How many newtons will it take to accelerate the object 1 meter in 1 second? $F = (\underline{\hspace{1cm}}$ kg • $\underline{\hspace{1cm}}$ m)/ $\underline{\hspace{1cm}}$ s² $F = \underline{\hspace{1cm}}$

6. An object has a mass of 10 kilograms. How many newtons will it take to accelerate the object 1 meter in 2 seconds? $F = (\underline{\hspace{1cm}}$ kg • $\underline{\hspace{1cm}}$ m)/ $\underline{\hspace{1cm}}$ s²

    $F = (\underline{\hspace{1cm}} \cdot \underline{\hspace{1cm}}) / \underline{\hspace{1cm}}$ $F = \underline{\hspace{1cm}} / \underline{\hspace{1cm}}$ $F = \underline{\hspace{1cm}}$

Name: _____ Date: _____

Dynes

Dynes are also a unit of force. Dynes are a smaller unit of force than newtons. One hundred thousand dynes equals one newton (100,000 dynes = 1 newton). An object with one gram is attracted to the earth's center with a force of 980 dynes. A **dyne** is the force needed to accelerate one gram one centimeter per second squared.

1 gram = 980 dynes	100,000 dynes = 1 newton
1,000 grams = 1 kilogram	1 kilogram = 9.8 newtons

Solve the following.

	Grams		Dynes
1.	1	=	980
2.	2	=	_____
3.	3	=	_____
4.	5	=	_____
5.	10	=	_____
6.	50	=	_____
7.	100	=	_____
8.	1,000	=	_____

Name: _____   Date: _____

More Volume and Density

Now we know about matter, mass, and weight. We know that matter is the amount of atoms in an object, and mass is the way to measure the matter in an object. Weight is the measurement of the force of gravity on the mass of the object. To take the measurements to the next level, we need to figure out volume and density.

Volume

As we learned earlier, volume is the measurement of how much space an object takes up. How can you find the volume of an object that is a certain shape? There are different formulas for finding the volume of different shapes. Let's list the formulas and then work through each of them separately.

Volume of Rectangular Prisms and Cubes

For three-dimensional figures like cubes and rectangular prisms (shapes like boxes) the formula is:
Volume = Length x Width x Height.
A cubic inch is 1 inch in length, 1 inch in width, and 1 inch high.

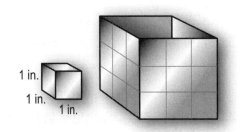

1 in.
1 in.
1 in.

Answer the following.

1. A cubic foot would be   a) 1,628   b) 1,728   c) 1,828   d) 1,928   cubic inches.

2. A cubic meter would be   a) 10,000   b) 50,000   c) 1,000,000   d) 2,000,000   cubic centimeters

3. A cubic yard would be   a) 27   b) 37   c) 47   d) 57   cubic feet.

When finding the volume of rectangular prisms and cubes, remember that the length, width, and height must be stated in the same units. If you are using inches, the width, length, and height all must be stated in inches. If you are using feet, the width, length, and height all must be stated in feet.

Example: The length of a figure is 6 inches, the width is 3 inches, and the height is 2 inches. Volume = 6 • 3 • 2. Volume = 36 cubic inches.

Name: _____ Date: _____

Match Column I with the correct volume in Column II.

_____ 1. Object 2 • 3 • 4 inches   A. 40 cubic feet

_____ 2. Object 4 • 2 • 5 centimeters   B. 24 cubic meters

_____ 3. Object 8 • 4 • 2 yards   C. 64 cubic yards

_____ 4. Object 2 • 3 • 4 meters   D. 24 cubic inches

_____ 5. Object 4 • 2 • 5 feet   E. 40 cubic centimeters

Find the volume.

1. The length of a box is 10 inches, the width is 5 inches, and the height is 3 inches.

   Volume = length • width • height   Volume = _____ • _____ • _____

   Volume = _____ cubic _____.

2. The length of a rectangular prism is 5 feet, the width is 4 feet, and the height is 1 foot.

   Volume = length • width • height   Volume = _____ • _____ • _____

   Volume = _____ cubic _____.

3. The length of a box is 8 yards, the width is 4 yards, and the height is 2 yards.

   Volume = length • width • height   Volume = _____ • _____ • _____

   Volume = _____ cubic _____.

4. A box is 5 centimeters in length, 2 centimeters in width, and 1 centimeter in height.

   Volume = length • width • height   Volume = _____ cm • _____ cm • _____ cm

   Volume = _____ cm³ (cubic centimeters)

5. A box is 20 centimeters in length, 4 centimeters in width, and 2 centimeters in height.

   Volume = _____ • _____ • _____   Volume = _____ cm³

6. A crate is 3 meters in length, 2 meters in width, and 2 meters in height.

   Volume = _____ • _____ • _____   Volume = _____ m³

7. A large box is 4 yards in length, 3 yards in width, and 4 yards in height.

   Volume = _____ • _____ • _____

   Volume = _____ cubic   a) feet   b) meters   c) yards.

8. A crate is 5 feet in length, 6 feet in width, and 3 feet in height.

   Volume = _____ • _____ • _____   Volume = _____ cubic _____.

   This same crate in inches is _____ in. long, _____ in. wide, and _____ in. high.

   The volume in cubic inches is   a) 1,550   b) 15,520   c) 155,520.

9. A box is 2 meters in length, 2 meters in width, and 1 meter in height.

   Volume = _____ • _____ • _____   Volume = _____ cubic _____.

   This same crate in centimeters is _____ cm in length, _____ cm in width, and

   _____ cm in height. Volume = _____ • _____ • _____. Volume = _____ cm³.

Name: _____ Date: _____

Volume of Spheres

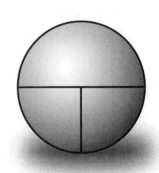

Objects shaped like a ball are called **spheres**. To find the volume of a sphere, use the formula: $(4/3)\pi \cdot r^3$. We already learned that r = the radius of the sphere. π is the symbol for **pi. Pi is a special number that is 22/7, which is a number without end. It is often shortened to $\approx$ 3.14.** The **diameter** is the distance through the center of the sphere from one surface to the other surface. The **radius** is one-half the diameter.

Let's work on each part of this formula separately.

Complete the following using the diagram of the sphere above.

1. Place the letter "c" on the solid circle. This line is the **circumference** of the sphere. The circumference is the distance around the sphere.

2. Place the letter "d" on the line that goes from one side of the circle to the other. This line is the **diameter** of the sphere. It is the distance across the circle through the center of the sphere.

3. Place the letter "r" on the line that goes from the center to the edge of the circle. This line is one **radius** of the sphere. The radius of the circle is the distance from the center of the sphere to the circumference. The radius is one-half as long as the diameter.

Solve the following for r^3. r = radius of sphere

4. $r = 2$ $r^3 = 2^3$ $= 2 \cdot 2 \cdot 2 = $ _____

5. $r = 3$ $r^3 = 3^3$ $= 3 \cdot 3 \cdot 3 = $ _____

6. $r = 4$ $r^3 = 4^3$ $= 4 \cdot 4 \cdot 4 = $ _____

7. $r = 5$ $r^3 = 5^3 = $ _____ $\cdot$ _____ $\cdot$ _____ $= $ _____

8. $r = 6$ $r^3 = $ _____ $= $ _____ $\cdot$ _____ $\cdot$ _____ $= $ _____

Solve the following for $\pi \cdot r^3$. $\pi \approx 3.14$
(Round each decimal to nearest whole number)

9. $3.14 \cdot 2^3 = 3.14 \cdot$ _____ $= $ _____ $= $ _____ (nearest whole number)

10. $3.14 \cdot 3^3 = 3.14 \cdot$ _____ $= $ _____ $= $ _____ (nearest whole number)

11. $3.14 \cdot 4^3 = 3.14 \cdot$ _____ $= $ _____ $= $ _____ (nearest whole number)

12. $3.14 \cdot 5^3 = 3.14 \cdot$ _____ $= $ _____ $= $ _____ (nearest whole number)

13. $3.14 \cdot 8^3 = 3.14 \cdot$ _____ $= $ _____ $= $ _____ (nearest whole number)

Name: _____ Date: _____

Find the volume for these spheres.

Example: Find the volume of a ball with a radius of 2 inches ($r = 2$).

Formula: $4/3\pi \cdot r^3$

Step 1: $r^3 = 2^3 = (2 \cdot 2 \cdot 2) = 8$

Step 2: $3.14 \cdot 8 = 25.12 = 25$ (nearest whole number)

Step 3: cubic answer $\quad \dfrac{4}{3} \cdot \dfrac{25}{1} = \dfrac{100}{3} = 33.33$ cubic inches.

1. A sphere has a radius of 3 inches. Complete each step.

Step 1: $r^3 =$ _____^{3} = _____ • _____ • _____ = 27

Step 2: $3.14 \cdot 27 =$ _____ = _____ (nearest whole number)

Step 3: cubic answer $\quad \dfrac{4}{3} \cdot$ _____ = _____ = _____ cubic inches

2. A sphere has a radius of 4 feet. Complete each step.

Step 1: $r^3 =$ _____^{3} = _____ • _____ • _____ = 64

Step 2: $3.14 \cdot 64 =$ _____ = _____ (nearest whole number)

Step 3: cubic answer $\quad \dfrac{4}{3} \cdot$ _____ = _____ = _____ cubic feet

3. A sphere has a radius of 5 feet. Complete each step.

Step 1: $r^3 =$ _____^{3} = _____ • _____ • _____ = 125

Step 2: $3.14 \cdot$ _____ = _____ = _____ (nearest whole number)

Step 3: cubic answer _____ • _____ = _____ = _____ cubic _____

Name: _____ Date: _____

Density

You have learned that in some objects the atoms are packed very tightly. This makes the object very **dense**. In other objects, the atoms are not so tightly packed. The object is less dense. Bowling balls and foam balls are both made of matter. The matter (atoms) in the bowling ball is very dense. The matter (atoms) in the foam ball is not dense. As a result, the mass of the bowling ball is greater than the mass of the foam ball, and it weighs a great deal more too.

Density is a ratio used to express how much matter is in a given volume. For our purposes, we will treat mass and weight as the same to find the density of objects. The formula to measure density is **Density = mass/volume**. Density is measured in grams per cubic centimeter.

Cubic centimeter: 1 cm • 1 cm • 1 cm = 1 cm³

Example: The mass of an object is 4 grams (g).

The volume of the object is 8 cubic centimeters (cm³).

Density = mass/volume or D = m/v

D = 4/8   D = 0.5 or ½ gram per cubic centimeter

Find the density.

1. The mass of an object is 38.6 grams. The volume is 2 cubic centimeters.

   D = m/v   D = _____ g ÷ _____ cm³   D = 18.3 g/cm³ (grams per cubic centimeter)

2. The mass of an object is 23.4 g. The volume is 3 cm³.

   D = m/v   D = _____ g ÷ _____ cm³   D = 7.8 g/cm³

3. The mass of an object is 9 g. The volume is 9 cm³.

   D = m/v   D = _____ g ÷ _____ cm³   D = _____ g/cm³

4. The mass of an object is 10.8 g. The volume is 2 cm³.

   D = m/v   D = _____ g ÷ _____ cm³   D = _____ g/cm³

5. The mass of an object is 24 g. The volume is 4 cm³.

   D = m/v   D = _____ ÷ _____   D = _____ g/cm³

Name: _____ Date: _____

Buoyancy

We know how to find mass, weight, volume, and density. But how do these calculations apply in real life? Let's look at water. We already learned that when matter has less density than water, like a piece of wood, it will float. When an object has greater density, like a piece of lead, it will sink. But what exactly determines if an object will float or not? The scientific word for floating is buoyancy.

Buoyancy is the measurement of water pressure versus the weight of an object. The pressure of water becomes greater with the depth of the water. The water pressure increases 62.4 pounds for each one foot of depth. One foot below the surface, the water pressure is 62.4 pounds per each cubic foot of water. Two feet below the surface, the water pressure is 124.8 pounds per each cubic foot of water. A ping-pong ball floats on the surface of water. At one foot below the water, there is 62.4 pounds of pressure on the ball. The farther under the water you hold the ball, the greater the pressure. If the ping-pong ball is subjected to too much pressure, it will be crushed. However, water pressure doesn't just press down on objects. Water pressure is exerted in all directions. So while you may be able to crush a ping-pong ball if you put it under enough water pressure, the reason the ball floats in the first place is also water pressure. When an object is placed in water, the **water pressure is an upward force** against the object. This upward force is a **buoyant force**. The buoyant force works against the object sinking.

The **weight of the object is a downward force** into the water. The downward force works to make the object sink. When an object is more dense and heavier than an equal volume of water, the object will sink. If an object is less dense than an equal volume of water, the buoyant force is greater and the object will float. Remember, the way to calculate density is mass divided by volume.

Find the density of water, cork, and iron.

Density = mass ÷ volume or D = m/v

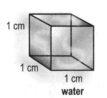

1 cm

1 cm

1 cm

water   cork   iron

1. Water has a mass of 3 grams per 3 cubic centimeters (cm³).

   D = _____ / _____ = 3 ÷ 3 = 1   D = _____ g/cm³

2. Cork has a mass of 1 g per 4 cm³.

   D = _____ / _____ = 1 ÷ 4 = _____   D = _____ g/cm³

3. Iron has a mass of 31.5 grams per 4 cm³.

   D = _____ / _____ = _____ ÷ ____ = _____   D = _____ g/cm³

4. The density of a cubic centimeter of water is (greater / less) than a cubic centimeter of cork. The cork will (float / sink) in water.

5. The density of a cubic centimeter of iron is (greater / less) than a cubic centimeter of water. The iron will (float / sink) in water.

Name: _____ Date: _____

Displacement: Sink or Float?

An object will sink until it displaces an amount of water equal to its weight. **Displacement** was discovered by Archimedes. Archimedes noted that, upon climbing into a bathtub full of water, the level of the water rose according to the weight of the object placed in it. In other words, an object that has greater density than the fluid into which it is placed will sink. A less dense object will float. A cork floats in water because water is more dense than cork. The cork displaces its weight in water long before it sinks. The density for one cubic centimeter (cm^3) of each of the objects below is given. Water density is 1 gram per cm^3.

Place the letter "F" on the blank if the object will float in water. Place the letter "S" on the blank if the object will sink in water.

D = 0.75 g/cm³   D = 3.0 g/cm³   D = 0.9 g/cm³   D = 15 g/cm³   D = 60 g/cm³

1. _____   2. _____   3. _____   4. _____   5. _____

When an object is placed in water, the object displaces an amount of water equal to the weight of the object. There is a buoyant force pushing up on the object. If the force of buoyancy is greater than its weight, an object will float. Some objects float much higher than others. Cork floats higher than most wood. The density of some woods is greater than others. Therefore, all wood does not float at the same level. The pieces of wood a, b, and c below are floating in water.

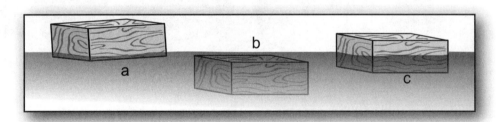

6. The piece of wood having the greatest buoyancy is _____.

7. The piece of wood with the least buoyancy is _____.

8. The piece of wood with the least density is _____.

9. The piece of wood with the greatest density is _____.

10. The volume of a cork is such that if fully submerged, it would displace 20 oz. of water. When one-fourth submerged, it displaces _____ oz. of water. The fraction part of the cork that will float out of the water is   a) $\frac{1}{4}$ b) $\frac{1}{2}$ c) $\frac{3}{4}$.

Name: _____ Date: _____

Density of Steel and Water

The density of steel is much greater than the density of water. A solid piece of steel that is 5 feet long, 4 feet wide, and 2 feet high has a volume of 5 ft. • 4 ft. • 2 ft. = 40 ft.³. The weight of steel is about 488 pounds per cubic foot. An equal volume of water is 40 ft.³. The weight of water is 62.4 pounds per cubic foot.

Answer the following.

1. The weight of the 5 ft. • 4 ft. • 2 ft. piece of steel can be found by multiplying volume by 488.

    W = _____ • _____   W = _____ pounds

2. The weight of the 5 ft. • 4 ft. • 2 ft. volume of water can be found by multiplying volume by

    62.4. W = _____ • _____ W = _____ pounds

3. The piece of steel will   a) float.   b) sink.

4. The piece of steel will sink until it displaces _____ pounds of water.

Buoyancy and Ships

Indian tribes along the Great Lakes had different ways of making canoes. Some made canoes of birch bark placed over a wooden frame. Others made canoes from hollowed-out logs. Use the diagram to answer the questions below.

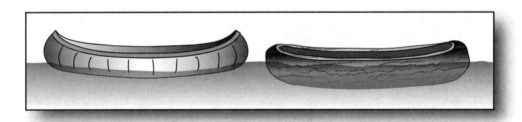

1. The canoe that displaced the greater amount of water was the

    a) birch-bark canoe.   b) hollowed-out log canoe.

2. The canoe that was most buoyant was the

    a) birch-bark canoe.   b) hollowed-out log canoe.

3. The amount of water displaced shows that the

    a) birch-bark canoe   b) hollowed-out log canoe   was lighter in weight.

4. It would take more force to move the

    a) birch-bark canoe.   b) hollowed-out log canoe.

Name: _____ Date: _____

     Canoes made out of wood can clearly float on water because wood has a lower density than water. However, modern ships today aren't usually made out of wood. An aircraft carrier is made out of steel. How can it float?

     What if the 5 ft. • 4 ft. • 2 ft. = 40 ft.³ piece of steel from our earlier example is hollowed out? Then it weighs only one-tenth of its original weight. It is now like a steel ship, only much smaller.

Answer the following.

5. The weight of the hollowed-out piece of steel is $\frac{1}{10}$ of 19,520 pounds, which is

    a) 195   b) 1,952   pounds.

6. The piece of steel will displace _____ pounds of water.

7. The piece of hollowed-out steel will   a) float.   b) sink.

8. The piece of hollowed-out steel will float because an equal volume of water weighs

    a) more.   b) less.

     A water pressure force equal to the volume of water displaced is the buoyant force on an object in water. The water density weight is 62.4 lbs./ft³. The formula for finding the buoyant force is $F_{buoyant} = -D_{fluid}Vg$. This equation says that the buoyant force is equal to the density of the fluid times the volume of the object submerged times standard gravity. Standard gravity can be calculated just like finding a newton. The negative sign is needed because buoyancy moves in a direction opposite that of gravity.

     This principle applies as the size of the object gets larger. An aircraft carrier is huge, weighing in around 100,000 tons. But it is important to remember that, while 100,000 tons is extremely heavy, the ship is not solid. There are vast spaces in the interior of the ship filled with air. The enclosed volume of air results in an average density that is lower than that of the water. The shape of the carrier's hull, or body, is also important. The hull is designed to place more weight on a narrow surface, so that as the ship is placed into the water, it displaces the water before it is completely submerged. Even more importantly, the aircraft carrier's weight is spread out over a large distance. Most carriers are around 2,000 feet long. That's almost seven football fields long! These three things combine to result in a lower density for the ship than the water.

Name: _____ Date: _____

Chapter V: Newton's Laws of Motion

Newton's First Law of Motion

Remember our old friend Sir Isaac Newton? Newton not only discovered the law of gravity, he also established that there were laws of motion that guided how and why things moved. In total, Newton came up with three laws that explained why things move the way they do.

Newton's First Law of Motion says an object resists a change in its motion. What does this mean? Well, it means two different things. First, it means that an object at rest will stay at rest, unless a force causes a change. That makes sense when you think of a ball. A ball will not move until you kick it.

Second, this law means that an object in motion will stay in motion unless some force causes it to change. Think of a ball. You kick the ball, and it begins to roll. If you kick the ball outside on the grass, it will probably roll about 20 feet and then stop. Why will it only roll about 20 feet? Because the grass slows it down by providing friction. If you kick the ball inside on the gym floor, it will probably roll a lot farther. Why will it roll farther in the gym? Because the floor is a lot smoother, and there is less friction. Now imagine if you kick the ball where there is <u>no</u> friction. The ball would roll forever! A rolling ball will keep rolling unless a force causes it to change. Friction is a force that causes the ball to change its motion. The ball stops rolling because of friction.

The First Law of Motion is also known as the **Law of Inertia**. Inertia is another way of saying an object will keep doing what it was doing. An object resists a change in motion because of the object's inertia. The ball will sit there forever because of its inertia. Because an object resists a change in motion, one must apply a force to change an object's motion. When you kicked the ball, you were applying force to change the motion.

An important part of the First Law of Motion is mass. Remember, mass is the amount of matter an object contains. An object with a greater mass resists a change in motion more than an object with a smaller mass. It is easier to kick a soccer ball weighing 2 kilograms than a bowling ball weighing 12 kilograms.

Solve the following.

Each of the four objects below has the same volume. Place the number 1 on the blank for the object with the greatest inertia. Then use the numbers 2, 3, and 4 for the next objects.
M = mass

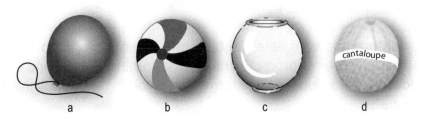

a   b   c   d

____ a. M = 1 ounce ____ b. M = 500 grams ____ c. M = 1 pound ____ d. M = 1 kilogram

Name: _____ Date: _____

Newton's Second Law of Motion

We now know that an object at rest will stay at rest, and an object in motion will stay in motion. Let's think back to our soccer and bowling balls again. When we tried to kick them, the soccer ball went much farther than the bowling ball. Why? This brings us to **Newton's Second Law of Motion**. The Second Law states that the force needed to move an object is equal to the product of that object's mass and acceleration. This is written as $F = ma$. Look familiar? That's also the formula for a newton.

Force here is often described as the **net force**. The net force is the sum of all the forces acting on an object. So think back to kicking the ball. When we kicked the ball outside on the grass, the grass was one force slowing down the ball. There was also air pressure and gravity. These are negative amounts that subtract from the total force. You subtract the force of friction, air pressure, and so on from the force moving the object, and this gives you the net force. Gravity is why it is important to consider the **mass** of the object. Again, the mass is the amount of matter in an object, and the more mass an object has, the more the pull of gravity makes it weigh. An object gains speed based on the size of the net force. The greater the net force, the greater the object gains in speed. A ball kicked in the gym goes farther than the ball kicked in the grass. An object also gains speed based on the mass of the object. The greater the mass, the slower the object gains speed. A soccer ball gains more speed than a bowling ball.

True or False.

_____ 1. Increase the net force on an object with a mass of 1 kilogram, and there is a gain in speed.

_____ 2. Increase the mass and maintain the same net force, and there is a gain in speed.

_____ 3. Decrease the net force on an object with the same mass, and there is an increase in speed.

_____ 4. Increase the net force on an object with the same mass, and there is an increase in speed.

_____ 5. Gain in speed and mass are inverses.

Speed and Velocity

We know that net force and mass affect the speed of an object. **Speed** is how fast an object is going. Speed can be measured by the following formula, $s = d/t$, where d equals distance traveled, and t = time. So when you kicked the ball outside in the grass, you achieved a speed of s = 20 ft. (d) ÷ 5 sec (t), or 4 ft. per second. The ball moved an average of 4 feet for every second it was moving. Velocity is a specific way of discussing speed. **Velocity** is speed in a particular direction. If the direction and speed of an object are given, velocity can be measured with a vector. Velocity measures a change in position over a period of time. If you kicked the ball in the grass to the right, it might move at 4 ft./sec. until it rolled to a stop. If you kicked the ball to the left, it might roll at 4 ft./sec. for 3 seconds and then hit a wall. Velocity measures the different speeds based on direction.

Name: _____ Date: _____

Answer the following.

If the statement is about speed, place the letter "S" on the blank. If the statement is about velocity, place the letter "V" on the blank.

_____ 1. The car was traveling at 50 miles per hour.

_____ 2. The car was traveling 50 miles per hour west.

_____ 3. They walked 4 miles per hour today.

_____ 4. They walked 4 miles per hour east and 3 miles per hour north.

_____ 5. The airplane flew 400 miles per hour toward the northwest.

Acceleration

When you kicked the ball in the grass, we figured that it rolled 20 ft. in 5 seconds, which was an average of 4 ft./sec. However, the ball did not move at exactly 4 feet every second. When you first kicked the ball, it moved faster than 4 ft. sec, but as the opposing force of the grass acted on it, the ball began to slow down. The scientific names for what happened to the speed of the ball are acceleration and deceleration. **Acceleration** is a change in velocity in a given time period. When you kicked the ball, it accelerated from 0 ft./sec to 8 ft./sec. In the first second, the ball traveled 8 feet. However, those opposing forces—friction from the grass, air pressure, and gravity—acted on the ball to slow it down. **Deceleration**, or negative acceleration, is slowing down the ball. In the final second the ball is rolling, it only rolls 2 ft./sec.

How does acceleration apply to velocity? Remember, velocity is a measure of the speed in a certain direction. So when you kick the ball in the grass to the right, it might accelerate from 0 ft./sec. to 8 ft./sec. and then, due to a decrease in net force, decelerate until it rolled 2 ft./sec. and then stopped. When you kick the ball to the left, it might accelerate from 0 ft./sec. to 8 ft./sec., decelerate to 6 ft./sec., and then hit the wall. Because you had different velocities, different speeds at different directions, you had different accelerations and decelerations.

True or False. Place a T on the blank if the statement is true or an F if the statement is false.

_____ 1. The velocity of an object depends on net force only.

_____ 2. The velocity of an object depends only on the mass of the object.

_____ 3. The velocity of an object depends on net force and the mass of the object.

_____ 4. Acceleration is a change in velocity in a period of time.

_____ 5. Speed tells you how fast an object is moving at a given time.

_____ 6. Acceleration tells how fast an object is moving and the direction in which it is moving.

_____ 7. When mass increases and the net force is maintained, the velocity decreases.

_____ 8. When net force is increased and the mass remains the same, the velocity increases.

Name: _____ Date: _____

Solve the following.

Increase in speed is in meters per second squared (m/s²). Increase in speed = Force/mass. Increase in speed = F ÷ m.

Find the increase in speed in meters per second squared (m/s²) for each of the following problems.

1. A force of 1 newton (N) is applied to a mass of 1 kilogram (kg). The increase in speed is found using Force/mass = increase in speed or F ÷ m = increase in speed.

    The force is _____ newton. The mass is _____ kilogram.

    1 N ÷ 1 kg/1²   Increase in speed = _____ meter per second

2. A force of 2 N is applied to a mass of 1 kg.

    The force is _____ newtons. The mass is _____ kilogram.

    2 N ÷ _____ kg/1² Increase in speed = _____ meters per second

3. A force of 8 N is applied to a mass of 1 kg.

    The force is _____ newtons. The mass is _____ kilogram.

    8 N ÷ _____ kg/1² Increase in speed = _____ meters per second

4. A force of 10 N is applied to a mass of 1 kg.

    The force is _____ newtons. The mass is _____ kilogram.

    _____ N ÷ 1 kg/1² Increase in speed = _____ meters per second

5. A force of 12 N is applied to a mass of 1 kg.

    The _____ is 12 _____. The _____ is 1 _____.

    _____ N ÷ 1 kg/1² Increase in speed = _____ meters per second

6. A force of 1 N is applied to a mass of 2 kg.

    1 N ÷ 2 kg/1² 1 N ÷ (2 ÷ 1)   Increase in speed = _____ meter per second

7. A force of 1 N is applied to a mass of 4 kg.

    1 N ÷ _____ kg/1² 1 N ÷ (4 ÷ 1)   Increase in speed = _____ meter per second

8. A force of 8 N is applied to a mass of 2 kg.

    8 N ÷ _____ kg/1² 8 N ÷ (_____ ÷ _____) Increase in speed = _____ meters per second

9. A force of 10 N is applied to a mass of 5 kg.

    10 N ÷ _____ kg/1² 10 N ÷ (5 ÷ 1) Increase in speed = _____ meters per second

10. A force of 12 N is applied to a mass of 4 kg.

    _____ N ÷ 4kg/1² 12 N ÷ (4 ÷ 1) Increase in speed = _____ meters per second

11. As the mass increases, the speed (increases / decreases).

12. Increasing the force (increases / decreases) the speed.

Name: _____ Date: _____

Complete the matching.

Match the term in Column A with the definition in Column B.

Column A	Column B
_____ 1. inertia	A. Amount of matter in an object
_____ 2. force	B. The change in velocity over a period of time
_____ 3. acceleration	C. Energy exerted to cause motion or a change in motion
_____ 4. net force	D. How fast an object is moving
_____ 5. mass	E. Resistance of an object to change in position
_____ 6. velocity	F. Sum of all of the forces acting on an object
_____ 7. speed	G. The speed and direction an object is moving

Speed and Distance of Falling Objects

Let's look at acceleration in falling objects. An object is dropped from a tall building. What are the net forces on this object? The only friction is from air pressure, and that is a constant. Gravity, which is usually a force for deceleration, here is working towards acceleration. Falling objects are pulled toward the earth's center by the force of gravity. This affects the speed of an object falling to Earth. The object's speed increases as it falls. The object's speed increases 9.8 meters each second. At the instant the object begins to fall, the speed is 0. So the mean speed for the first second is 4.9 meters per second (0 + 9.8/2). After the first second, the object's falling speed increases at a rate of 9.8 meters per second.

Solve the following.

Time	Speed
1. 1 second	4.9 meters per second
2. 2 second	4.9 + 9.8 = _____ meters per second
3. 3 second	14.7 + 9.8 = _____ meters per second
4. 4 second	24.5 + 9.8 = _____ meters per second
5. 5 second	34.3 + 9.8 = _____ meters per second

Answer the following.

6. After 1 second, the speed of the falling object is _____ meters per second.

7. After 2 seconds, the speed of the falling object is _____ meters per second.

8. After 3 seconds, the speed of the falling object is _____ meters per second.

9. After 4 seconds, the speed of the falling object is _____ meters per second.

10. After 5 seconds, the speed of the falling object is _____ meters per second.

Name: _____ Date: _____

11. Each second, the speed of the falling object increased _____ meters per second.

12. Complete the graph below for the object. Place a plus sign (+) on the chart for the speed at each second. The first + has been placed on the chart. Draw a line that connects the +'s.

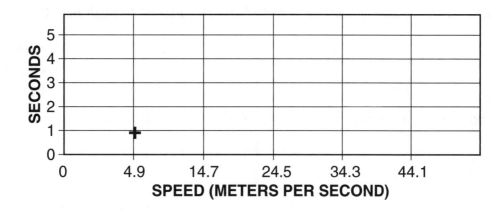

13. The graph tells you that the speed is increasing at a constant rate of _____ meters each second.

Distance an Object Falls

Now we know how gravity affects the speed of an object that falls. The next logical conclusion is that gravity also affects the distance an object will fall each second. We use the formula $d = \left[\frac{1}{2}(9.8 \text{ m/sec.})\right] \cdot t^2$, or $d = 4.9 \text{ m/sec.} \cdot t^2$

Solve the following.

1. When time (t) = 1 second, then t^2 = _____ • _____ = _____

2. When time (t) = 2 seconds, then t^2 = _____ • _____ = _____

3. When time (t) = 3 seconds, then t^2 = _____ • _____ = _____

4. When time (t) = 4 seconds, then t^2 = _____ • _____ = _____

5. When time (t) = 5 seconds, then t^2 = _____ • _____ = _____

6. When time (t) = 6 seconds, then t^2 = _____ • _____ = _____

7. When time (t) = 7 seconds, then t^2 = _____ • _____ = _____

8. When time (t) = 8 seconds, then t^2 = _____

9. When time (t) = 9 seconds, then t^2 = _____

10. When time (t) = 10 seconds, then t^2 = _____

Name: _____ Date: _____

Distance Chart

An object is dropped from the top of a building. Time is measured for each second from the instant the object is dropped. Distance is from the top of the building downward to the point where the object will land.

Complete the chart for the object as it falls from the top of the tall building.

Time Object Falls	Formula		Distance Object Falls in Meters
1. 1 second	$d = 4.9 \text{ m/sec.} \cdot t^2 =$	$d = 4.9 \cdot 1^2$	$d = 4.9 \cdot$ _____ $= \quad 4.9$ m
2. 2 seconds	$d = 4.9 \cdot t^2$ $=$	$d = 4.9 \cdot$ _____ ^{2}	$d = 4.9 \cdot 4 = \qquad$ _____ m
3. 3 seconds	$d = 4.9 \cdot t^2$ $=$	$d =$ _____ $\cdot$ _____ ^{2}	$d = 4.9 \cdot$ _____ $=$ _____ m
4. 4 seconds	$d = 4.9 \cdot t^2$ $=$	$d =$ _____ $\cdot$ _____ ^{2}	$d = 4.9 \cdot 16 = \qquad$ _____ m
5. 5 seconds	$d =$ _____ $=$	$d =$ _____ $\cdot$ _____ ^{2}	$d =$ ____ $\cdot$ ____ $=$ _____ m

6. Complete the graph below for the object. Place a plus sign (+) on the chart for each second and distance the object falls that second. The first + has been placed on the chart. Draw a line connecting the +'s.

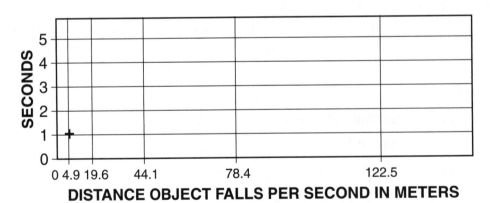

DISTANCE OBJECT FALLS PER SECOND IN METERS

7. The graph tells you that the distance the object falls

   a) is the same each second.   b) increases each second.

38

Name: _____   Date: _____

Newton's Third Law of Motion

Newton's Third Law of Motion states that for every action, there is an equal and opposite reaction. You may not notice the opposite reaction when you kick a ball on the grassy field, but let's say you decided to try to kick the ball while standing in the middle of an ice rink. The force it took for you to move the ball has an equal and opposite reaction in moving you. In the field, the force of your shoes on the grass would keep you from falling down. But if you were standing on ice, there is a much smaller force of friction on your shoes—ice is slippery! The equal and opposite reaction just might knock you off your feet. The Third Law is plainly visible in everyday life. When you go to step off a boat, the boat will float away in the water if you don't have it tied to the dock. When you try to kick a bowling ball to see how far it will roll, you will hurt your foot!

Write __T__ for True or __F__ for false.

1. _____   A bird is able to fly because of the Third Law of Motion.

2. _____   Without the Third Law of Motion, fish would never be able to swim anywhere.

3. _____   Another way to state the Third Law of Motion is that every time you push, you

    get pushed back.

4. _____   Newton's Third Law of Motion only applies on the surface of the earth.

5. _____   For the Third Law of Motion to work, you need three objects.

Name: _____ Date: _____

 # Chapter VI: Simple Machines

Work

The Meaning of Work

What is work? While you may think of work as everything from picking up your room to typing an essay, in science, work has a special meaning. **Work** is when an object moves in the same direction as the force acting on it. What does that mean? Well, when you kicked a soccer ball, the ball moved in the same direction you kicked it. You used work to move the ball. While typing the essay, you use work when you pressed down on the keyboard, but, in science, actually thinking of what to write is not work. For work to be done, an object must be moved in the same direction as the net force.

Complete the following.
Place a "W" on the blank by a statement if work has taken place. Place "NW" on the blank by a statement if no work has taken place. Place a plus sign (+) on the blank "A force was applied" and "Work was done" if those statements are true. Place a minus sign (–) on the blank if the statements are not true.

_____   1.   You push a box across the room.
                _____ A force was applied.   _____ Work was done.

_____   2.   You lift a sack of potatoes 5 feet.
                _____ A force was applied.   _____ Work was done.

_____   3.   You stand and hold a sack of flour.
                _____ A force was applied.   _____ Work was done.

_____   4.   You roll a large rock up a hill, but the rock rolls back to where
                you started pushing it.
                _____ A force was applied.   _____ Work was done.

Measuring Work

Remember, the definition of work is that force is applied to an object, and the object moves in the direction of the force. As with all the other concepts we have discussed so far, there is a way to measure the amount of work done. The amount of work can be found using the following formula: **Work = force • distance**. This formula says that to find the amount of work done, you must multiply force times distance. The net force and distance an object is moved must be in the same direction. The greater the distance you move an object, the more work you do. One can use force and not do any work. If you push against a wall and it doesn't move, you have not done any work. Work may be measured using the English system or the metric system.

Name: _____ Date: _____

Using the English System to Measure Work

In the English system, Work = force • distance ($W = f • d$) is used to measure work done. In the English system, force is in **pounds** and distance is in **feet**.

Answer the following.

1. In the English system, force is in   a) pounds.   b) distance.

2. In the English system, distance is in   a) meters.   b) feet.

3. In the English system, the amount of work is in   a) foot pounds.   b) newton meters.

Complete the following.

Place a plus sign (+) on the blank if work is done. Place a minus sign (–) on the blank if no work is done.

_____   4. A box weighs 40 pounds. You push the box 10 feet.

_____   5. A box weighs 50 pounds. You push the box 5 feet.

_____   6. A box weighs 100 pounds. You push the box 3 feet, and it slides back 4 feet.

_____   7. A motor is used to lift a 500-pound box from the floor. The box is raised 10 feet and placed in a truck.

_____   8. A motor is used to lift a 1,000-pound crate from the floor. The crate is raised 15 feet from the floor. The cable breaks, and the crate drops back 15 feet to the floor.

Find How Much Work   W = force • distance

9. A box weighs 30 pounds. You push the box 10 feet.

    $W = f • d$ W = _____ • _____   W = _____ ft. lbs.

10. A box weighs 60 pounds. You push the box 4 feet.

    $W = f • d$ W = _____ • _____   W = _____ ft. lbs.

11. A box weighs 100 pounds. You push the box 5 feet.

    $W = f • d$ W = _____ • _____   W = _____ ft. lbs.

12. A motor is used to lift a 300-pound box from the floor. The box is raised 10 feet.

    $W = f • d$ W = _____ • _____   W = _____ ft. lbs.

13. A motor is used to lift a 1,000-pound crate from the floor. The crate is raised 20 feet.

    $W = f • d$ W = _____ • _____   W = _____ ft. lbs.

Name: _____ Date: _____

Using the Metric System to Measure Work

In the metric system, force is measured in newtons and distance is in meters. As you may recall from previous chapters, another way of talking about force is to use the term newton. Therefore, in the metric system, units of work are newton/meters. There is a special term to describe newton/meters. A joule (J) = newton/meter or (Nm). A **joule** is the work done when a force of one newton moves an object one meter. Use the formula Work = force • distance.

Answer the following.

1. In the metric system, newton refers to   a) force.   b) distance.

2. In the metric system, meter refers to   a) force.   b) distance.

3. It takes 4 Nm to lift a small box 1 meter from the floor. The amount of work done is

   a) 1 joule.   b) 3 joules.   c) 4 joules.   d) 5 joules.

Find How Much Work   W = force • distance

4. It takes a force of 20 N (newtons) to push a box 10 m (meters).

   W = _____ N • _____ m   W = _____ joules

5. It takes a force 50 N to push a box 3 m.

   W = _____ N • _____ m   W = _____ joules

6. It takes a force of 400 N for a motor to lift a box 4 m.

   W = _____ N • _____ m   W = _____ joules

7. A large crane is used to lift a stone above the ground. It takes a force of 20,000 N to lift

   the stone 20 m.

   W = _____ N • _____ m   W = _____ joules

8. A boy lifts a bag of potatoes. It takes a force of 200 N to lift the bag to a height of 2 m.

   W = _____ N • _____ m   W = _____ joules

Equivalent Amounts of Work

The work done depends on the force used and the distance the object is moved. If you increase the force, it will take you less distance to do the same work.

   Example: Same amount of work in A and B.
      A. A greater force (power) does the work in a shorter distance.
         W = Fd   40 N • 5 m = 200 J (joules)

      B. A lesser force (power) takes a longer distance to do the work.
         W = Fd   20 N • 10 m = 200 J (joules)
         Same amount of work, but less force is used.

Name: _____ Date: _____

Complete the following.

In both "a" and "b" for each number, the same amount of work is done. Place numbers on the blanks so the work comes out the same for "a" and "b."

1. a) 100 N • _____ m = 400 J   b) 200 N • _____ m = 400 J

2. a) 600 N • _____ m = 1,800 J   b) 900 N • _____ m = 1,800 J

3. a) _____ N • 4 m = 1,200 J   b) 100 N • _____ m = 1,200 J

4. a) 500 N • _____ m = 2,000 J   b) _____ N • 5 m = 2,000 J

5. a) _____ N • 6 m = 1,500 J   b) 500 N • _____ m = 1,500 J

Power

     Say your mom asked you to carry a full laundry basket upstairs. You could do it two ways. You could take a deep breath, pick up the laundry, and run up the stairs as fast as possible. You would have done a lot of work in a short period of time. Or you could pick up the laundry basket and set it down on each step as you moved it up the stairs. Several minutes later, you reach the top of the stairs. In both cases, you would have done the same amount of work, but it would have taken a different amount of time. As you can see, a given amount of work may be done quickly. The same amount of work may be done over a longer period of time. In both cases, the amount of work is the same. The net force may not be the same, but the amount of work is the same.

     When we measure how long it takes to do work, we are actually talking about power. **Power** is how much work is done in a given period of time. It is how long it takes to complete a given amount of work. So when you ran up the stairs with the laundry basket, you were using more power than when you moved the basket up one step at a time. The amount of work was the same, but the time it took to do the work was different. We use the formula **P = (Force • Distance)/time** or **P = W/t** to measure power.

Find the power.

1. It takes a force of 40 pounds to push a box. You push the box 10 feet. It takes 2 minutes

    to move the box. $P = (\text{Force} • \text{Distance})/\text{time}$

    $P = (40 • 10)/2 =$ _____ ft. lbs./ _____ min. = _____ ft.lbs. per minute

2. It takes a force of 60 pounds to push a box. You push the box 5 feet. It takes 4 minutes to

    move the box.

    $P = ($_____ • _____$)/$ _____   = _____ ft. lbs./ _____ min.

    = _____ ft. lbs. per minute

Name: _____ Date: _____

3. It takes a force of 100 pounds to push a crate. You push the crate 10 feet. It takes 5 minutes to move the crate.

    $P = ($_____ • _____$)/$ _____   = _____ ft. lbs./ _____ min.

    $=$ _____ ft. lb. per minute

4. A motor uses a force of 500 pounds to lift a box from the floor. The box is raised 10 feet. It takes 20 seconds to raise the box.

    $P = ($_____ • _____$)/$ _____   = _____ ft. lbs./ _____ sec.

    $=$ _____ ft. lb. per second

5. A motor uses a force of 1,600 pounds to lift a crate from the floor. The crate is raised 10 feet from the floor. It takes 40 seconds to lift the crate.

    $P = ($_____ • _____$)/$ _____   = _____ ft. lbs./ _____ sec.

    $=$ _____ ft. lb. per second

Simple Machines

Long ago, the only way to do work was to push and pull. But then people began to think of better ways to do the same thing. For example, it used to be that the only way to move a large rock was to lift it, but that was very difficult to do. Then someone had an idea. They noticed that if a long rod or stick were placed under the rock, and a smaller rock placed under the stick, they could use less work to move the rock. This stick and rock combination is called a lever, and is an example of a simple machine. A machine is something that makes work easier by changing the work applied to the machine. There are six kinds of simple machines. In addition to the **lever**, the other simple machines are the **wedge**, the **screw**, the **wheel and axle**, the **inclined plane**, and the **pulley**.

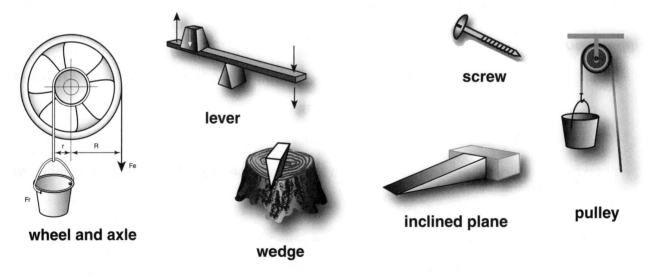

wheel and axle

lever

wedge

screw

inclined plane

pulley

Name: _____ Date: _____

Mechanical Advantage

The purpose of simple machines is to help one work. Simple machines make it easier to do work. A machine helps you conserve the total amount of work done. For example, let's say you agree to help your dad move to a new office on the first floor in a new building. You start to carry boxes up the six steps to the first floor, but then you notice that everyone else is using the wheelchair-accessible ramp. At first, it doesn't make sense. You have to walk much farther on the ramp than you would to go up the six steps. But the ramp is an example of an inclined plane. The angle of the ramp decreases the force needed to lift objects, like boxes, over the distance you are lifting them. In other words, it takes less work to walk the extra distance of the ramp carrying the box than it does to lift the box while climbing the stairs.

An inclined plane, the wheelchair-accessible ramp from our earlier example, is a simple machine. It helps you do work. There is a gain in work when using a simple machine. The work gain is also called the **mechanical advantage**. The mechanical advantage is the number of times a machine multiplies the force needed to do the work. It is the advantage gained by using a machine instead of using only one's own strength. To find out how much advantage is gained by using a simple machine, you use the formula "resistance force divided by the effort force."

Mechanical Advantage = resistance force divided by the effort force
$$MA = F_r \div F_e$$

Solve for Mechanical Advantage (MA).

1. $F_r = 8$ $F_e = 2$ MA = _____

2. $F_r = 15$ $F_e = 3$ MA = _____

3. $F_r = 27$ $F_e = 9$ MA = _____

4. $F_r = 48$ $F_e = 12$ MA = _____

5. $F_r = 121$ $F_e = 11$ MA = _____

When calculating the mechanical advantage of a simple machine, the greater the number, the greater the advantage of using the simple machine. In other words, bigger numbers make it easier for you to do work.

6. Which of the above machines had the greatest mechanical advantage? _____

7. Which had the smallest mechanical advantage? _____

Name: _____ Date: _____

Levers

Remember moving the rock with a lever? **Levers** are often used for mechanical advantage. Using a lever balanced on a fulcrum, or fixed point, makes it easier to move an object. There are three kinds of levers. A first-class lever is like a seesaw. The fulcrum is between the effort force (you) and the resistance (your classmate). A second-class lever is like a wheelbarrow. The resistance (the dirt) is between the fulcrum (the wheel) and the force (you). A third-class lever is like a fishing pole. The force (your upper hand) is between the resistance (the fishing lure) and the fulcrum (your lower hand).

First-class levers are widely used. When you use force to push down on one side of the lever, the resistance, or load, moves up. The closer the load is to the fulcrum, the less force it takes to lift it. Think of a lever as two parts, even though it is one object. On one side of the fulcrum is the resistance arm. The resistance, or load, is on this side of the fulcrum. On the other side of the fulcrum is the effort arm. This is the side that you push on to move the load. Remember, our formula for finding the mechanical advantage is $MA = F_r \div F_e$. Applied to levers, the formula is transformed into $MA = $ Effort Arm $\div$ Resistance Arm.

Example: The lever is 9 feet long. The fulcrum is between the resistance arm and effort arm. The resistance arm is 3 feet long; the effort arm is 6 feet long.

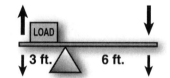

$$MA = \textbf{E-arm} \div \textbf{R-arm}$$
$$MA = 6 \div 3$$
$$MA = 2$$

If we took the same length lever, 9 feet, and moved the fulcrum a foot closer to the load, the mechanical advantage would change. The resistance arm is now 2 feet long, and the effort arm is now 7 feet long.

$$MA = \textbf{E-arm} \div \textbf{R-arm}$$
$$MA = 7 \div 2$$
$$MA = 3.5$$

There is a greater mechanical advantage when the fulcrum is closer to the load.

Find the mechanical advantage for the following first-class levers.

1. R-arm = 2 feet, E-arm = 4 feet. The ratio of the arms is _____ to _____. MA = _____

2. R-arm = 4 feet, E-arm = 12 feet. The ratio of the arms is _____ to _____. MA = _____

3. R-arm = 1 foot, E-arm = 5 feet. The ratio of the arms is _____ to _____. MA = _____

4. R-arm = 5 feet, E-arm = 15 feet. The ratio of the arms is _____ to _____. MA = _____

5. R-arm = 3 feet, E-arm = 6 feet. The ratio of the arms is _____ to _____. MA = _____

6. Which of the above levers had the greatest mechanical advantage? _____

7. Which had the smallest mechanical advantage? _____

Name: _____ Date: _____

Inclined Planes

The **inclined plane** is a simple machine that makes work easier. Moving an object up a slope is easier than lifting it straight up. The length of the slope will vary. The height may also vary. To find the mechanical advantage, the length (slope) must be divided by the height.

Example: The slope of the inclined plane is 10 feet. The height is 2 feet.

MA = slope ÷ height
MA = 10 ÷ 2
MA = 5

H = 2 feet   Slope = 10 feet

Again, remember that the larger the number, the greater the mechanical advantage. So what happens when the length of the slope is increased to 12 feet while the height remains 2 feet?

MA = slope ÷ height
MA = 12 ÷ 2
MA = 6

12 ft.   2 ft.

This is why wheelchair-accessible ramps are so long. The longer the ramp, the less work it takes to maneuver up it.

Find the mechanical advantage for the following inclined planes.

1. Slope = 30 feet, height = 10 feet MA = _____

2. Slope = 20 feet, height = 5 feet MA = _____

3. Slope = 15 feet, height = 3 feet MA = _____

4. Slope = 12 feet, height = 2 feet MA = _____

5. Slope = 20 feet, height = 2 feet MA = _____

6. Which of the above inclined planes had the greatest mechanical advantage? _____

7. Which had the smallest mechanical advantage? _____

Name: _____ Date: _____

Solve the following.

The inclined planes in 8, 9, 10, and 11 below all have the same height. The length (slope) is different for each. Mechanical advantage = slope ÷ height

8.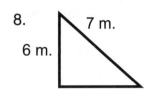

9.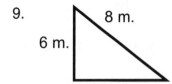

10.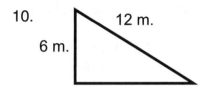

11.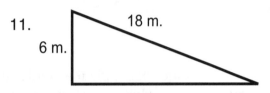

8. Mechanical Advantage = _____ ÷ _____ MA = a) $1\frac{1}{6}$ b) 2   c) $2\frac{1}{2}$ d) 3

9. Mechanical Advantage = _____ ÷ _____ MA = a) 1   b) $1\frac{1}{3}$ c) 2   d) $2\frac{1}{3}$

10. Mechanical Advantage = _____ ÷ _____ MA = a) $\frac{1}{2}$ b) 1   c) $1\frac{1}{2}$ d) 2

11. Mechanical Advantage = _____ ÷ _____ MA = a) 1   b) 2   c) 3   d) 4

12. When height remains the same, there is an increase in mechanical advantage when the

    slope length is (longer / shorter).

Solve the following.

The inclined planes in 13, 14, 15, and 16 below all have different slopes and heights.
Mechanical advantage = slope ÷ height   slope = length

13. 6 m. 2 m.

14. 8 m. 4 m.

15. 18 m. 6 m.

16. 24 m. 3 m.

13. Mechanical Advantage = _____ ÷ _____ MA = a) $\frac{1}{2}$ b) 1   c) 2   d) 3

14. Mechanical Advantage = _____ ÷ _____ MA = a) $\frac{1}{2}$ b) $1\frac{1}{2}$ c) 2   d) $2\frac{1}{2}$

15. Mechanical Advantage = _____ ÷ _____ MA = a) 2   b) 3   c) 9   d) 12

16. Mechanical Advantage = _____ ÷ _____ MA = a) 4   b) 6   c) 8   d) 10

Name: _____ Date: _____

Screws

A **screw** is a simple machine much like the inclined plane. One way to think of a screw is to envision it as an inclined plane wrapped around a cylinder. Here, the inclined plane forms the threads of the screw. The distance between threads on the screw is called the **pitch**. One complete turn of the screw moves the screw into an object a distance equal to the pitch. So if you are using a screw with a pitch between screw threads of $\frac{1}{8}$ inch to attach a knob to the cabinet, then one complete turn of the screw moves the screw $\frac{1}{8}$ inch into the cabinet.

Pitch is the distance from one thread to the next thread.

If the pitch of the screw threads is close together, then the screw must be turned more times than if it is spaced farther apart. The closely spaced threads are like making an inclined plane longer. When the screw threads are farther apart, then the screw must be turned fewer times. When screw threads are farther apart, it is like making an inclined plane steeper.

Solve the following.

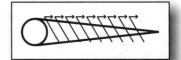

In each of the following, a force is used to place a screw in wood. In each case, the screw is one inch long.

1. The distance between the threads is $\frac{1}{8}$ inch. This means that each complete turn of the screw will move the threads _____ inch into the wood.

2. The distance between the threads is $\frac{1}{10}$ inch. This means that each complete turn of the screw will move the threads _____ inch into the wood.

3. The distance between the threads is $\frac{1}{4}$ inch. This means that each complete turn of the screw will move the threads _____ inch into the wood.

4. The distance between the threads is $\frac{1}{16}$ inch. This means that each complete turn of the screw will move the threads _____ inch into the wood.

Compare the screws above to inclined planes.

5. If the screws in #1 and #4 were inclined planes, the steeper plane would be _____.

6. If the screws in #2 and #3 were inclined planes, the steeper plane would be _____.

The steeper the screw pitch, the greater the force for a complete turn.

7. A screw with $\frac{1}{8}$ inch pitch would require (more / less) force for one complete turn of the screw than a screw with $\frac{1}{16}$ inch pitch.

8. A screw with $\frac{1}{16}$ inch pitch would require (more / less) force for one complete turn of the screw than a screw with $\frac{1}{4}$ inch pitch.

Name: _____   Date: _____

Wedges

A **wedge** is a simple machine that is a kind of inclined plane. However, a wedge differs in that it has two sloped sides, while an inclined plane has only one. Common wedges include knives, axes, needles, and nails.

To find the mechanical advantage for a wedge, divide the length of the slope by the thickness at the larger end of the wedge. Use the formula **Mechanical Advantage = slope ÷ thickness**.

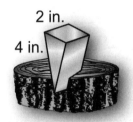

2 in.

4 in.

Example: You have a wedge for splitting chunks of firewood that has a slope of 4 inches and is 2 inches thick at the end.

$MA = s \div t$
$MA = 4 \div 2$
$MA = 2$

Remember, the larger the number, the greater the mechanical advantage. So if we have another wedge that has a slope of 6 inches and is 2 inches thick at the end, the formula changes to this:

$MA = s \div t$
$MA = 6 \div 2$
$MA = 3$

Find the mechanical advantage for the following wedges.

1. Slope: 6 inches   Thickness: 3 inches $MA =$ _____

2. Slope: 8 inches   Thickness: 2 inches $MA =$ _____

3. Slope: 10 inches   Thickness: 5 inches $MA =$ _____

4. Slope: 4 inches   Thickness: 1 inch $MA =$ _____

5. Slope: 5 inches   Thickness: $\frac{1}{2}$ inch $MA =$ _____

6. Which of the above wedges had the greatest mechanical advantage? _____

7. Which had the smallest mechanical advantage? _____

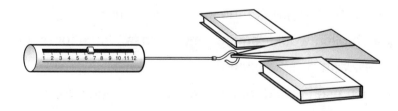

Name: _____ Date: _____

Wheel and Axle

Considered by many to be humankind's greatest invention, the wheel is everywhere in our daily lives. Wheels are on cars, bikes, and trucks. But did you know that a screwdriver is also a wheel and axle? It's true. How? It is not merely the circular wheel that makes this simple machine work, but its combination with an axle. An axle is basically a small circle inside a larger circle so they turn on the same axis. Think of the wheel on a bicycle. When you pedal, the bicycle chain is turning a small axle on the inside, which then turns the larger wheel with the tire on it. Imagine if your bicycle chain had to go the whole diameter around the larger wheel. Pedaling would be a nightmare! With a screwdriver, the handle is a large wheel, and the shaft is a smaller axle. Your effort in turning the handle makes the wheel travel a greater distance than the axle does.

Wheels and axles are circles. It is the size of the circles that is key to finding the mechanical advantage. To find the mechanical advantage for a wheel and axle, the ratio of the radius of the wheel to the radius of the axle must be found. The radius is one-half the distance through the center of a circle. The formula for this is **Mechanical Advantage = *r*(wheel) ÷ *r*(axle)**.

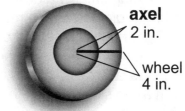

axel
2 in.

wheel
4 in.

Example: wheel radius = 4 in.
axle radius = 2 in.
MA = *r*(wheel) ÷ *r*(axle)
MA = 4 ÷ 2
MA = 2

This means that in one complete turn of this wheel and axle, the distance the wheel travels is two times greater than the distance the axle travels. Remember, the larger the number, the greater the mechanical advantage. So if the radius of our wheel is six inches and the axle is two inches, the formula would look like this:

MA = *r*(wheel) ÷ *r*(axle)
MA = 6 ÷ 2
MA = 3

This tells us that the smaller the axle is when compared to the size of the wheel, the greater the mechanical advantage.

Find the mechanical advantage for the following.

MA = radius of wheel ÷ radius of axle   *MA* = *r*(wheel) ÷ *r*(axle)

1. Wheel radius = 40 inches, axle radius = 10 inches.

    The ratio of the wheel to the axle is _____ to _____, or 4 to _____.

    MA = _____. In one turn, the wheel will travel _____ times farther than the axle.

Name: _____ Date: _____

2. Wheel radius = 10 inches, axle radius = 2 inches.

   The ratio of the wheel to the axle is 10 to _____, or 5 to _____.

   MA = _____. In one turn, the wheel will travel _____ times farther than the axle.

3. Wheel radius = 36 inches, axle radius = 3 inches.

   The ratio of the wheel to the axle is _____ to _____, or _____ to _____.

   MA = _____. In one turn, the wheel will travel _____ times farther than the axle.

Gears

Gears are a special kind of wheel and axle. Gears are wheels with teeth. The teeth are located around the circumference of the gears. The teeth of the gears must be spaced so that when the wheels turn, the teeth mesh together. A mechanical advantage can be gained by using gears. The advantage is larger when the gears are not the same size. The smaller gear, with its corresponding smaller diameter, will turn more times in a given period of time than the gear with the larger diameter. As a result, the smaller gear turns faster.

When two gears work together, one is the input gear. This is also called the drive gear. The **input gear** is connected to the source of the effort. When the input gear has a smaller diameter than the output gear, it makes the larger gear turn more slowly. When the input gear has a larger diameter than the output gear, the smaller gear will complete more rotations. The smaller gear turns faster.

Solve the Following.

Larger Input Gear

1. The input gear has 16 teeth. The smaller output gear has 8 teeth. The larger input gear makes one complete turn. The smaller gear will make   a) 1   b) 2   c) 3   d) 4   complete turns.

2. The input gear has 24 teeth. The smaller output gear has 8 teeth. The larger input gear makes one complete turn. The smaller gear will make   a) 1   b) 2   c) 3   d) 4   complete turns.

3. The input gear has 36 teeth. The smaller output gear has 12 teeth. The larger input gear makes two complete turns. The smaller gear will make   a) 2   b) 4   c) 6   d) 8   complete turns.

4. The input gear has 48 teeth. The smaller output gear has 8 teeth. The larger input gear makes three complete turns. The smaller gear will make   a) 8   b) 12   c) 16   d) 18   complete turns.

Name: _____ Date: _____

Smaller Input Gear

5. The input gear has 8 teeth. The larger output gear has 16 teeth. The smaller input gear makes one complete turn. The larger gear will make   a) $\frac{1}{4}$ b) $\frac{1}{2}$ c) $\frac{3}{4}$ d) 1 complete turn.

6. The input gear has 12 teeth. The larger output gear has 48 teeth. The smaller input gear makes one complete turn. The larger gear will make   a) $\frac{1}{4}$ b) $\frac{1}{2}$ c) $\frac{3}{4}$ d) 1 complete turn.

7. The input gear has 12 teeth. The larger output gear has 16 teeth. The smaller input gear makes two complete turns. The larger gear will make   a) $\frac{3}{4}$ b) 1   c) $1\frac{1}{2}$ d) 2 complete turn.

8. The input gear has 16 teeth. The larger output gear has 48 teeth. The smaller input gear makes one and one-half complete turns. The larger gear will make a) $\frac{1}{4}$ b) $\frac{1}{2}$ c) $\frac{3}{4}$ d) 1   complete turn.

    Gear ratio is comparing one gear size to another. The ratio can be found by comparing the number of teeth on gears. The ratio can also be found by comparing the radius of the gears. An input gear has 16 teeth. The output gear has 8 teeth. The ratio is 16:8, or 2:1. Similarly, the diameter of the input gear is 9 inches, and the diameter of the output gear is 3 inches. The ratio is 9:3, or 3:1.

Find the gear ratio for each of the following by using the number of teeth.

1. The input gear has 24 teeth. The output gear has 8 teeth.
    The gear ratio is   a) 2:1   b) 3:1   c) 4:1   d) 5:1

2. The input gear has 24 teeth. The output gear has 12 teeth.
    The gear ratio is   a) 2:1   b) 3:1   c) 4:1   d) 5:1

3. The input gear has 32 teeth. The output gear has 8 teeth.
    The gear ratio is   a) 2:1   b) 4:1   c) 6:1   d) 8:1

4. The input gear has 60 teeth. The output gear has 12 teeth.
    The gear ratio is   a) 3:1   b) 4:1   c) 5:1   d) 6:1

Find the gear ratio for each of the following by using the radius.

5. The input gear has a diameter of 12 inches. The output gear has a diameter of 6 inches.
    The gear ratio is   a) 2:1   b) 3:1   c) 4:1   d) 5:1

6. The input gear has a diameter of 20 inches. The output gear has a diameter of 4 inches.
    The gear ratio is   a) 2:1   b) 3:1   c) 4:1   d) 5:1

7. The input gear has a diameter of 30 inches. The output gear has a diameter of 5 inches.
    The gear ratio is   a) 4:1   b) 5:1   c) 6:1   d) 7:1

8. The input gear has a diameter of 5 inches. The output gear has a diameter of 5 inches.
    The gear ratio is   a) 1:1   b) 2:1   c) 3:1   d) 4:1

Name: _____ Date: _____

Torque

Gears use torque to gain a mechanical advantage. **Torque** is a twisting force that turns something. You use torque to help tighten a bolt with a wrench. The longer the wrench, the greater the torque. In the English system, torque force is measured in foot pounds, or inch pounds. In the metric system, torque force is measured in newton-meters. To find torque using foot pounds, or inch pounds, you multiply the length of radius of the gear by the pounds of force applied to the gears. Similarly, to find the torque in newton-meters, you multiply the length of the radius of the gears by the force in newtons.

Torque = radius of gear • force

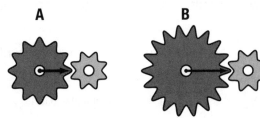

→ Radius

⚙ Output gear (turning gear)

⚙ Input gear (drive gear)

Find the torque in foot-pounds.

1. Four pounds of force are applied to an input gear with a radius that is two feet in length. The torque is   a) 2   b) 4   c) 6   d) 8   foot pounds.

2. Four pounds of force are applied to an input gear with a radius that is one foot in length. The torque is   a) 2   b) 4   c) 6   d) 8   foot pounds.

3. Five pounds of force are applied to an input gear with a radius that is two feet in length. The torque is   a) 10   b) 12   c) 14   d) 16   foot pounds.

4. Three pounds of force are applied to an input gear with a radius that is two feet in length. The torque is   a) 2   b) 4   c) 6   d) 8   foot pounds.

5. Two pounds of force are applied to an input gear with a radius that is 0.5 feet in length. The torque is   a) 1   b) 2   c) 3   d) 4   foot pounds.

Find the torque in newton-meters.

6. Four newtons of force are applied to an input gear with a radius that is one meter in length. The torque is   a) 4   b) 6   c) 8   d) 10   newton-meters.

7. Two newtons of force are applied to an input gear with a radius that is two meters in length. The torque is   a) 4   b) 6   c) 8   d) 10   newton-meters.

8. One newton of force is applied to an input gear with a radius that is seven meters in length. The torque is   a) 3   b) 7   c) 9   d) 10   newton-meters.

9. Eight newtons of force are applied to an input gear with a radius that is three meters in length. The torque is   a) 16   b) 24   c) 30   d) 32   newton-meters.

10. Three newtons of force are applied to an input gear with a radius that is 0.5 meters in length. The torque is   a) $\frac{1}{2}$ b) 1   c) $1\frac{1}{2}$ d) 2   newton-meters.

Name: _____ Date: _____

Pulleys

A **pulley** is a kind of lever that changes the direction of a force and/or multiplies the force. All pulleys involve two parts. To be a pulley, a simple machine must have a rope or belt wrapped around a wheel. Pulleys can be set up in three different ways: a single fixed pulley, a movable pulley, and a block and tackle system. In a **single fixed pulley**, the load moves up as the force applied to the rope moves down. A **movable pulley** is set up so that the force and load move in the same direction. A **block-and-tackle system** combines a fixed pulley working with a movable pulley. This system changes the direction of the force and multiplies the force.

A Single Fixed Pulley 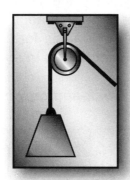  **A Movable Pulley**

What does all that mean? Well, let's say your Aunt Gertie wanted to move a grand piano into her second-floor bedroom (Aunt Gertie always was a little strange). The piano is too big to carry up the stairs. Now, the movers could just stand on the second floor and lift using a 100-foot rope, but a grand piano weighs about 1,000 pounds. So the movers decide to use a pulley. Which pulley will make lifting the piano to the second floor the easiest? A single fixed pulley uses one 100-foot rope but still requires 1,000 pounds of force to lift the piano. It might seem a little easier on the movers because now they would be pulling down with gravity instead of up. However, since there is only one rope, there is no mechanical advantage. A movable pulley is better, because it would add a mechanical advantage of two, since there are two rope segments supporting the movable pulley. The movers would have to lift 1,000 pounds of piano using 500 pounds of effort to pull on 200 feet of rope.

However, with a block-and-tackle pulley, the movers can get a considerable mechanical advantage. By combining a fixed pulley with movable pulleys, the 1,000 pounds of the piano is now divided between the pulleys. If the movers added a third pulley, the 1,000 pounds would be divided again over three pulleys with four ropes, so it would be

Name: _____ Date: _____

like lifting 250 pounds. The more pulleys you add to a block-and-tackle system, the easier it is to lift the weight. The only down side is that for every pulley, you have to double the rope. With two pulleys, the movers would need 200 feet of rope, and with three pulleys, 400 feet of rope. If they used 4 pulleys, it would be like lifting 125 pounds, but they would need 800 feet of rope to do it!

The mechanical advantage for a block-and-tackle system is found by counting the number of rope segments in the system that are suspending the weight. When the movers decided to use three pulleys to get Aunt Gertie's grand piano up to the second floor, they had four rope segments—one attached to the beam sticking out above the window, two between the first fixed pulley and the moving pulley, and one between the moving pulley and the second fixed pulley. That is a mechanical advantage of four. The rope segment you pull on doesn't count, because it is not suspending the weight. So the formula for using a block-and-tackle system is **Mechanical advantage = number of rope segments in system holding weight.**

Find the mechanical advantage for the following block-and-tackle systems.

a.

b.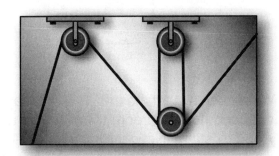

1. Pulley "a" has _____ ropes moving it.

2. Pulley "a" has a MA of   a) 2.   b) 3.   c) 4.   d) 5.

3. Pulley "a" would lift a 200-kg box using an effort of

    a) 50   b) 100   c) 150   d) 200   kg.

4. Pulley system "b" has _____ ropes moving it.

5. Pulley system "b" has a MA of   a) 2.   b) 3.   c) 4.   d) 5.

6. Pulley system "b" would lift a 200-kg box using an effort of

    a) 50   b) 100   c) 150   d) 200   kg.

7. Pulley system "b" would lift a 1,000-kg box using an effort of

    a) 100   b) 150   c) 200   d) 250   kg.

8. A pulley system like "b" lifts an object with an effort of 100 kg. The weight of the object is

    a) 200   b) 400   c) 600   d) 800   kg.

Name: _____ Date: _____

Chapter VII: Vectors

As you have no doubt figured out by now, math is an important part of physical science. We have already seen how properties such as mass and density can be determined using mathematical equations and variables. Let's look at how mathematics is used to help identify and define vectors, an important concept of physical science.

Scalar and Vector Measurement

Vectors are made up of two parts. The parts are magnitude and direction. **Magnitude** is a number that indicates the distance. **Direction** is a course taken, such as east, west, north, or south. A vector indicates how far something travels in a specific direction.

When you take away direction, you no longer have a vector. Instead, you now have a scalar. A **scalar** is a number without direction. Weight is a scalar. Your height is a scalar. Even speed is a scalar. Scalars do not need direction to define them.

How can speed be a scalar? Let's think of a car. When you are driving to the store, you can describe your trip with a vector. Your car has a speed, and that speed is traveling northeast, in the direction of the store. You drive past the repair shop, where Mr. Jones is trying to fix the speedometer of a car. He has that car up on blocks and the accelerator depressed. The car is reaching speeds of 55 miles per hour, but it is not going anywhere. The car has speed, but no distance and direction, so the 55 miles per hour is a scalar.

Place the letter "S" on the blank if the statement is a scalar. Place the letter "V" on the blank if the statement is a vector.

_____ 1.   The box weighs 5 pounds.

_____ 2.   The temperature is 68°.

_____ 3.   The car is traveling north at 30 miles per hour.

_____ 4.   The airplane is flying southwest at 200 miles per hour.

_____ 5.   It is now 5:00 p.m.

_____ 6.   A car is traveling at 40 miles per hour.

_____ 7.   A car is traveling at a velocity of 40 miles per hour east.

_____ 8.   The temperature is 45 degrees.

_____ 9.   The package weighed 2 pounds.

_____ 10. The plane flew 400 miles per hour northeast.

Name: _____ Date: _____

Magnitude and Direction of Vectors

Vectors are often represented with arrows. These arrows are shown with an end, which represents the starting point of the vector. The arrows also have a head, which is the point of the arrow. This shows the direction of the vector. Frequently, the length of the arrow is scaled to show the magnitude of the vector. When a vector is scaled to show the magnitude, a specific scale is used. For example, one inch on the vector equals five miles in real life.

Solve the following.

1. Measure the arrow below. Each inch = 2 miles.

   ———————————————▶

   The length of the arrow is   a) 2   b) 4   c) 6   d) 8   miles.
2. Measure the arrow below. Each inch = 2 kilometers.

   ———————————▶

   The kilometer length is   a) 2   b) 4   c) 6   d) 8   kilometers.
3. Measure the arrow below. Each centimeter = 2 miles. (Each inch = 2.54 centimeters.)

   ———————————————————————▶

   The centimeter length is   a) 2.54.   b) 5.08.   c) 10.16.   d) 12.7.
4. Measure the arrow below. Each inch = 5 meters.

   ——————————▶

   The meter length is   a) 5.   b) 7.5.   c) 8.5.   d) 10.

Solve the following.

For each of the vectors below, the scale is shown. Measure each vector and choose the correct answers for each.

5. Each inch is 100 miles. This vector is   a) 1   b) 2   c) 3   d) 4   inch(es).
   This vector represents   e) 40   f) 100   g) 200   h) 300   miles.

   ————————▶

6. Each centimeter is 50 miles. This vector is   a) 1   b) 2   c) 3   d) 4   centimeter(s).
   This vector represents   e) 50   f) 100   g) 200   h) 300   miles.

   ——————————————▶

7. Each inch is 5 meters. This vector is   a) 1   b) 2   c) 3   d) 4   inch(es).
   This vector represents   e) 15   f) 20   g) 25   h) 30   meters.

   ———————————————————▶

Name: _____ Date: _____

8. Each centimeter is 4 kilometers. This vector is   a) 2   b) 4   c) 6   d) 8 centimeters.
    This vector represents   e) 6   f) 12   g) 18   h) 24   kilometers.

    ——————————————→

9. Each inch is 10 feet. This vector is   a) 3   b) 5   c) 7   d) 9   inches.
    This vector represents   e) 30   f) 40   g) 50   h) 60   feet.

    ——————————————————————→

The Coordinate System

We have learned that vectors are used to show direction. Without direction, there is no vector. Vectors can be shown as north, south, east, or west. For example, on the coordinate system below, vector "a" is pointing east. Vector "b" is pointing north.

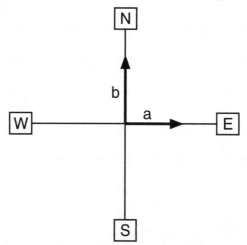

Vectors are measured counterclockwise on the coordinate system. For example, in the diagram below, vector "a" would be north of east. Vector "b" would be north of west. Vector "c" would be south of west. Vector "d" would be southeast.

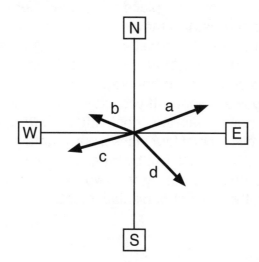

Name: _____ Date: _____

Use the coordinate system map below and answer the questions that follow.

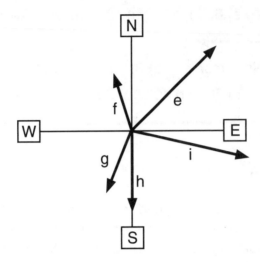

1. Vector "e" is pointing   a) north of west. b) northwest. c) northeast.   d) southwest.

2. Vector "f" is pointing   a) west of north. b) northeast. c) west of south. d) southeast.

3. Vector "g" is pointing   a) west of north. b) northeast. c) west of south. d) southeast.

4. Vector "h" is pointing   a) west of north. b) south.   c) west of south. d) southeast.

5. Vector "i" is pointing   a) west of north. b) southeast. c) south of east. d) west of south.

Displacement

Remember displacement? As we learned in Chapter 4, for an object to float, it must displace an amount of water equal to its weight. Let's look at displacement in more detail. **Displacement** is movement from one place to another place. For an object to float, it must move a certain amount of water from one place to another. Remember floating a ship on the sea? When the ship goes into the water, it moves, or displaces, an amount of water equal to its weight. But when the ship comes out of the water, the water returns to its normal levels. Just by looking at the water, you could not tell a boat had ever been in it.

How can you apply this concept to other areas of physical science? Displacement works this way in other areas of physical science. If you leave home and walk two blocks to school, it is displacement. If you leave home, walk to school, and then return home after school, it is not displacement. You traveled a distance of four blocks, but your total displacement was zero. That does not mean you did not go to school. But by measuring with displacement, the two blocks you walked to school were canceled out by the two blocks you walked home from school. Vectors can be used to show the amount of displacement.

Name: _____ Date: _____

Use diagram "A" and "B" below to answer the questions.

Place a plus sign (+) on the blank next to the correct statement.

1. An individual in "A" walks from "a" and returns to "a."

    _____ displacement   _____ no displacement

2. An individual in "B" walks from "a" and stops at "c."

    _____ displacement   _____ no displacement

A
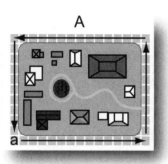

B
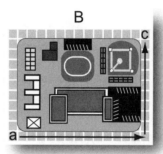

Vectors measuring displacement are a straight line. However, when measuring displacement, frequently the displacement does not occur in a straight line. Then you must use multiple vectors to measure the displacement.

> ***Example:*** You leave your home and walk 100 meters east. What is your displacement?
> Scale: Each inch = 50 meters

Start here ⎯⎯⎯⎯⎯⎯⎯⎯⎯▶ End here
East

Your displacement is 100 meters east.
Then you walk 50 meters north.

To find your displacement, add the vectors.
Your displacement is 150 meters northeast.

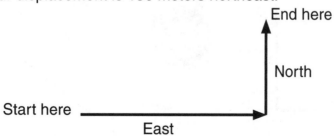

As you can see, when measuring displacement, direction often changes. A new vector measures the new direction. To find the total displacement, you add the vectors together.

Name: _____ Date: _____

To find your displacement for the shortest route ("c" in the right triangle below), you find the vector distance for "c." Because the vectors make a right triangle, you can use the following formula to find the hypotenuse of the right triangle, which is "c."

$$c = \sqrt{a^2 + b^2}$$

$c = \sqrt{100^2 + 50^2}$ $c = \sqrt{10,000 + 2,500}$ $c = \sqrt{12,500}$ $c \approx 111$ meters

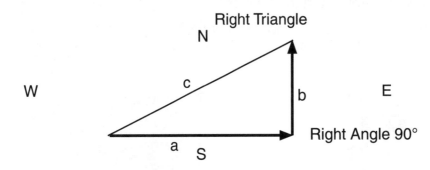

Right Triangle

Find the displacement for each of the following.

Starting point = ●, stopping point = ○.

A. Scale: one inch = 1 mile

B. Scale one-half inch = 1 kilometer

3. The displacement in "A" is   a) 2 miles east.   b) 5 miles east.

4. The displacement in "B" is   a) 3 kilometers northeast.   b) 5 kilometers northwest.

C. Scale 1 centimeter = 1 meters

D. Scale: 1 centimeter = 5 kilometers

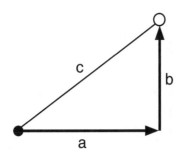

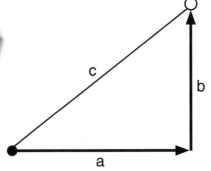

Name: _____ Date: _____

5. Adding the vectors for "c," the displacement is   a) 7 meters northeast.

    b) 7 meters north.

6. Use the formula $c = \sqrt{a^2 + b^2}$ to find the direct distance on "c" from start to stop:

    a) 5 meters.   b) 7 meters.

7. Adding the vectors for "d," the displacement is   a) 9 kilometers northeast.

    b) 45 kilometers northeast.

8. Use the formula $c = \sqrt{a^2 + b^2}$ to find the direct distance on "d" from start to stop:

    a) 32+ meters.   b) 45+ meters.

Speed or Velocity?

    While you may think of them as the same, remember, speed and velocity are different. Speed is a scalar number. **Speed** is the distance traveled in a certain amount of time. The formula for speed is ***Speed = distance ÷ time***. Speed is written as miles per hour or kilometers per hour.

    Velocity is a vector. It has a number and a direction. **Velocity** is change in position over a period of time. It is speed in a particular direction. The formula for velocity is ***Velocity = change in position ÷ change in time***. Velocity is written as miles per hour, direction; or kilometers per hour, direction.

    Joe is going to spend the night with a friend. He decides to jog to the friends's home. He leaves his home and jogs at a rate of 5 miles per hour toward the northeast. Joe has a velocity of 5 miles per hour and a northeast direction. Joe stops at his friend's home and spends the night. Joe's jogging is a velocity because there is a change in position from his starting point.

    During the winter, Joe finds it too cold to jog outside, so he jogs at the gym. Joe still maintains his speed of 5 miles an hour, but he never goes anywhere. He never leaves the same spot on the treadmill. He has a speed of 5 miles an hour, but no velocity. His speed of 5 miles an hour is a scalar because there is no direction.

Name: _____ Date: _____

Complete the following.

If the following situation is a speed only, place a plus sign (+) on that statement. If the situation is a velocity, place a plus sign (+) on that statement.

1. He was walking at a speed of 3 miles per hour.

   _____ This is a speed problem because it has no direction.

   _____ This is a velocity problem because there is speed and direction.

2. We drove at an average speed of 55 miles per hour.

   _____ This is a speed problem because it has no direction.

   _____ This is a velocity problem because there is speed and direction.

3. The airplane was flying northeast at a velocity of 350 kilometers per hour.

   _____ This is a speed problem because it has no direction.

   _____ This is a velocity problem because there is speed and direction.

4. The wind was blowing at a velocity of 30 miles per hour from the southwest.

   _____ This is a speed problem because it has no direction.

   _____ This is a velocity problem because there is speed and direction.

5. The runner won the race with a speed of 3 minutes 42 seconds.

   _____ This is a speed problem because it has no direction.

   _____ This is a velocity problem because there is speed and direction.

Acceleration

You probably experience acceleration many times every day. You may know that when the car you are riding in begins to go faster, it is accelerating. **Acceleration** is a vector quantity that is defined as the rate at which an object changes its velocity. Remember, velocity is a change in position over time. Our jogger, Joe, had a constant velocity of 5 miles per hour. He changed his position 5 miles for every hour he jogged. When Joe accelerates, he is changing his velocity.

While Joe jogs toward the northeast, he jogs at a velocity of 5 miles per hour for 15 minutes. Then, for 30 minutes, he increases his velocity from 5 miles per hour to 6 miles per hour. Then, he finishes his jog by increasing his velocity to 7 miles per hour for the final 15 minutes. Joe has been accelerating his velocity as he jogs.

Name: _____ Date: _____

Answer the following.

In each of the following situations, there is velocity. Place the letter "V" on the blank if there is velocity but no acceleration. Place the letter "A" on the blank if there is acceleration.

_____ 1. The plane's velocity was a constant 300 miles per hour for the entire 5 hour flight.

_____ 2. The motorbike was traveling at a constant velocity of 40 miles per hour.

_____ 3. Each hour the increase in velocity for the plane was 50 miles per hour.

_____ 4. Each hour the increase in velocity for the motorbike was 3 to 5 miles per hour.

Average Rate of Acceleration

Acceleration is the rate of change in velocity. A car is traveling southeast at 50 miles per hour. Then the car speeds up for over a period of three hours to a speed of 70 miles per hour. The velocity of the car was 50 miles per hour/southwest. Then the velocity changed to 70 miles per hour/southwest. When the car's velocity changed from 50 to 70 miles per hour/southwest, it accelerated.

To find the average rate of acceleration, subtract the initial velocity from the final velocity. Then divide that number by the time. For example, subtract the initial (beginning) velocity of the car (50 mph) from the final (ending) velocity (70 mph). This gives you 20 mph. Now divide that by the time it took to reach the final velocity (3 hours). The result is 6.67 mph/h. The car was accelerating at a rate of 6.67 mph/h.

$$\text{Average acceleration} = \frac{\text{final velocity} - \text{initial velocity}}{\text{elapsed time}} \quad \text{or} \quad a = \frac{V_f - V_i}{t}$$

Find the average rate of acceleration for the following situations.

1. A long-distance runner is running at a velocity of 5 miles per hour/west. In the next two hours, he increases his velocity to 7 miles per hour/west. His average rate of acceleration is _____ mph per hour.

2. A jet is flying at a velocity of 500 kilometers per hour/east. Over a period of 4 hours, the pilot increases the velocity to 700 kilometers per hour/east. The average rate of acceleration is _____ kph per hour.

Name: _____ Date: _____

3. Susan is driving her car at a velocity of 50 miles per hour/northeast. Over a 3-hour period, she increases to a velocity of 65 miles per hour/northeast. The average rate of acceleration is _____ mph per hour.

4. Joe is running a 5,000-meter race. He runs the first 1,000 meters at a velocity of 5.5 meters per second/west. In sixty seconds, he increases his velocity and is running 1,000 meters at a velocity of 7 meters per second/west. The average rate of acceleration is _____ meters per second per second.

5. A paper airplane is flying through the air at a velocity of 4 meters per second/southwest. A gust of wind pushes it to a velocity of 6 meters per second/southwest over a period of 4 seconds. The average rate of acceleration is _____ meter per second per second.

Acceleration Vectors and Direction

Remember, acceleration is a vector, and vectors must have a direction. So far, we have talked about acceleration as a forward direction. The scientific term for that forward movement is **positive acceleration**, and not surprisingly, it is written as +. Have you already figured out what the opposite of positive acceleration is? If you guessed negative acceleration, written with a −, you are correct!

Joe is jogging at a constant speed of 5 miles per hour. He accelerates to a speed of 6.5 miles per hour in order to catch up to his friend Jorge. Jorge is jogging at a constant speed of 5 miles per hour. Joe catches up to Jorge and slows his speed from 6.5 miles per hour to 5 miles per hour and jogs with Jorge. When Joe slowed down to 5 miles per hour, this 'slowing down' is known as **negative acceleration**. Negative acceleration is also known as **deceleration**. Joe's acceleration from 6.5 to 5 miles an hour was in the opposite direction from his motion.

It may be difficult to think of slowing down as acceleration, but remember the scientific definition of acceleration. Acceleration is a vector quantity that is defined as the rate at which an object changes its velocity. Joe is changing his velocity in a positive direction up to minute 4. Then Joe's change in velocity goes in a negative direction from minute 4 to 5. This is negative acceleration or deceleration.

Time (min.)	Velocity (mph)
0	0
1	2
2	3
3	5
4	6.5
5	5
6	5

Name: _____ Date: _____

Use the table below to answer the following.

Billy is testing out his new bike. The following chart shows his acceleration.

Time (min.)	Velocity (mph)
0	0
1	5
2	10
3	15
4	10
5	5
6	0

1. Billy's rate of positive acceleration from minute 1 to minute 2 is

    a. 1 mile per hour per minute.   b. 3 miles per hour per minute.

    c. 6 miles per hour per minute.   d. 5 miles per hour per minute.

2. Billy's rate of negative acceleration from minute 4 to minute 5 is

    a. 1 mile per hour per minute.   b. 3 miles per hour per minute.

    c. 6 miles per hour per minute.   d. 5 miles per hour per minute.

3. When did Billy begin to slow down?

    a. After 3 minutes.   b. After 2 minutes.

    c. After 4 minutes.   d. After 5 minutes.

4. Billy's rate of acceleration was

    a. the same each minute.   b. changing each minute.

Name: _____ Date: _____

Chapter VIII: Static Electricity

Electrical Charge in Atoms

Has this ever happened to you? You slide across a car seat, touch the car door, and get shocked. This is an example of **static electricity**. Static electricity is a spark of electricity that is generated by electrons jumping from one atom to another. It is called static because it is not flowing. As we will see in the next chapter, electricity has a current. Static electricity is electricity at rest. It has no current.

As we already learned earlier in the book, all objects are made of tiny pieces called atoms. Every atom is made up of electrons, protons, and neutrons. We use the Bohr Model to describe atoms. The nucleus is the center of the atom, just like the sun. Protons and neutrons make up the nucleus of the atom. The protons and neutrons are held very tightly in the nucleus of an atom. **Neutrons** do not have a charge; they are neutral. The **protons** have a positive (+) charge. The Bohr Model shows the electrons in orbit around the nucleus, like planets. The **electrons** have a negative charge (–). Under ideal circumstances, there are equal numbers of protons and electrons. The positive and negative charges are balanced, and the atom is neutral.

Label the parts of the atom below with the following terms.

neutrons	protons	nucleus	electrons

1.

a. _____

b. _____

c. _____

d. _____

When we discussed atoms earlier, we focused on the protons. Remember, the number of protons in the nucleus is what gives the atom its identity. The number of protons never changes. But electrons are another story.

Electrons may move from atom to atom. They can do this when two objects come into contact with each other. Rubbing increases the amount of contact between two objects. Some things hold electrons better than others. Plastic, glass, and cloth are examples of materials that hold electrons. These are commonly referred to as **insulators**. Other things let electrons

Name: _____ Date: _____

move more freely. Most metals let electrons move freely. These are commonly referred to as **conductors**. What happens to the atom when it gains or loses electrons? When atoms lose electrons, the atoms have more protons than electrons. The atoms are no longer balanced, and they have a positive charge. If atoms gain electrons, they have more electrons than protons, and the atoms have a negative charge. In both cases, an atom with a charge is no longer referred to as an atom, but is now called an **ion**.

So as we have seen, static electricity is caused by electrons moving from one atom, or group of atoms, to another atom, or group of atoms. Two negatively charged objects will **repel**, or move away from, each other. Two positively charged objects will also repel each other. Two objects with unlike charges will **attract**, or move closer to, each other. This happens more than you might be aware of. Have you seen the effects of negatively charged objects repelling or attracting other objects in real life? Well, if your socks have ever stuck together when they came out of the dryer, then you have seen attraction between a negatively charged object and a positively charged one. What happens is that, as clothing is tumbled in the dryer, electrons are rubbed off some clothes and onto others. When the clothes stop spinning, the electrons try to seek balance by attaching to a positively charged shirt. Dryer sheets and fabric softeners reduce this static electricity by giving each object a thin chemical coating that prevents the electrons from attaching during all that tumbling.

If you have brushed your hair in the winter only to find that your hair is now standing straight out, you have seen repelling in action. When you brush your hair, some electrons are rubbing off your hair and onto the brush. Each of your hairs now has a positive charge, so they try to move away from each other, resulting in a bad hair moment. That's why misting your hair with water, rubbing a small amount of lotion on your hands and then through your hair, or spritzing a bit of hairspray on the brush keeps your hair in place. All of those things provide a barrier to keep the electrons from jumping ship.

Let's look at this in action. When a rubber rod is rubbed with a silk cloth, the silk cloth loses electrons. The rubber rod gains electrons. The silk cloth then has a positive (+) charge, and the rubber rod has a negative (–) charge. When a glass rod is rubbed with a silk cloth, the glass rod loses electrons. The glass rod then has a positive (+) charge. The silk cloth gains electrons, and the cloth then has a negative (–) charge.

Complete the following.

2. Below are a glass rod and a rubber rod. Both rods have been rubbed with a silk cloth. Place the symbol for negative charge (–) on the ends of the rod that has become negatively charged. Place the symbol for positive charge (+) on the ends of the rod that has become positively charged.

Glass Rod

Rubber Rod

Name: _____ Date: _____

The dark rods below are made of rubber, and the light rods are made of glass. The rods have been rubbed with a silk cloth. Complete the activities that follow.

A. Rubber rod   ▬▬▬▬▬▬▬▬   Rubber rod   ▬▬▬▬▬▬▬▬

B. Rubber rod   ▭▭▭▭▭▭▭▭   Glass rod   ▬▬▬▬▬▬▬▬

C. Glass rod   ▭▭▭▭▭▭▭▭   Glass rod   ▭▭▭▭▭▭▭▭

3. Place the negative symbol (–) on each end of the rod set that would be negatively charged.

4. Place the positive symbol (+) on each end of the rod set that would be positively charged.

5. Place the positive (+) and negative (–) symbols on the rod set that would have both charges.

6. The rubber rods in Set A would   a) repel   b) attract   each other.

7. The rubber rod and glass rod in Set B would   a) repel   b) attract   each other.

8. The glass rods in Set C would   a) repel   b) attract   each other.

Place a plus sign (+) beside the activity if it would produce static electricity.

_____ 9.   Rubbing a glass rod with a silk cloth

_____ 10. Rubbing a rubber rod with a silk cloth

_____ 11. Rubbing a rock with a silk cloth

_____ 12. Sliding across a car seat

_____ 13. Touching a doorknob after walking across carpet

Grounding

When you build up a negative charge after walking across a carpet, the electrons need someplace to go. If you touch the doorknob, the electrons will jump to the doorknob and eventually travel through the floor and back into the ground. It turns out that the earth is a huge conductor, so electrons will seek a path that leads to the ground.

Grounding is a safety feature that provides a path for electrons to return to the ground. There are certain wires in the electrical wiring of your house that lead to the ground. You can also ground yourself by touching a metal object that is in contact with the ground.

Grounding is an important part of everyday life. That spark you see from static electricity could destroy your computer or even start a fire. While that little shock you feel may seem like a minor irritation, it is actually capable of doing much greater damage. Electronics, like computers, MP3 players, televisions, and more are all powered by electricity. Too much electricity

Name: _____ Date: _____

could literally fry their circuits, erasing all your files, pictures, and songs. Similarly, if you discharge too much static electricity around a flammable substance, like gasoline at a gas station, you could actually start a fire.

This is why you should ground yourself before touching things that could be damaged by static electricity. Before you turn on your computer, you should touch something metallic. By discharging all your extra electrons before you turn on your computer, you have made sure that your computer won't be the conductor.

Similarly, when you go with your parents to get gas for the lawn mower, there are many signs around the gas station telling you to take the gas can out of the car and set it on the ground before filling it. Why? Well, you probably put the gas can in the trunk of your car to go to the gas station, and it probably shifted around on the carpeting during the drive. The gas can probably picked up some extra electrons. By setting the gas can on the ground, you are grounding it, eliminating the chance of having a spark jump from the can to the gas.

Complete the following.

Place a G on the items that would ground an object. Place an NG on the items that would not ground an object.

_____ 1. Rubbing a glass rod with a silk cloth

_____ 2. Touching the car hood after you get out of it

_____ 3. Using a paperclip to turn off a light switch

_____ 4. Sliding across a car seat

_____ 5. Touching a door knob after walking across carpet

Humidity and Static Electricity

Have you noticed that you tend to shock yourself more during the winter than the summer? Why is that? The answer is that it depends on the humidity. **Humidity** is the amount of water vapor the air is holding. Air with a higher humidity has more water vapor. Air with a humidity of 75% has more water vapor than air with 25% humidity. The higher the percentage, the greater the humidity. More water vapor means that the air will allow electron buildup to dissipate more rapidly. Water is a conductor of electricity, so more water in the air means that the electrons can move more freely on their own. In high humidity, the electrons do not need you to help them move around.

In the winter, there is lower humidity in the air. Cold air cannot hold as much water vapor as warm air, so the humidity is lower in the cooler months. This means that electrons cannot move as freely from negatively charged surfaces to positively charged surfaces and must rely on an additional conductor, you, to move around.

How can you avoid shocking yourself during the winter? There are several ways to prevent accidental static discharges. First, increase the humidity in your house. That will automatically reduce the amount of static buildup. Next, ground yourself frequently. No, I don't mean send yourself to your room as punishment, but instead, release any additional electrons you are

Name: _____ Date: _____

building up by touching a conductive surface every few minutes. If you know you have to walk across a carpeted room, touch the doorknob before you start, the metal lamp halfway across the room, and the light switch on the other side. By regularly discharging your electrons, you avoid a larger, cumulative shock. Finally, move slowly. As we learned earlier, rubbing increases the contact that leads to electron exchange. If you move slowly, you allow the electrons to naturally leave you. Hold your hand about an inch from the doorknob and count to 15. By then, enough electrons will have already moved from you to the doorknob that you will get little, if any, shock.

Complete the following.

Place a check by the humidity levels that would increase your chances of static electricity discharge.

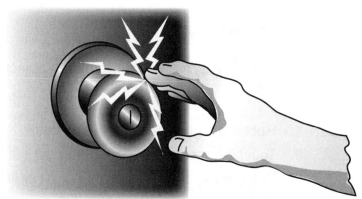

_____ 1. 15%

_____ 2. 45%

_____ 3. 93%

_____ 4. 78%

_____ 5. 26%

Circle the best choice.

6. To reduce your chances of getting shocked by static electricity, you should (increase / decrease) the humidity in your home.

7. You will get more static shocks if you (reduce / increase) your electron buildup.

8. By (frequently / rarely) touching conductive surfaces, you can reduce your electron buildup.

9. Moving (slowly / quickly) will increase your electron buildup, and possibly lead to more static shocks.

10. Most people experience static electricity more in the (winter / summer).

Name: _____ Date: _____

Lightning

Lightning is similar to the spark from static electricity. However, lightning is a much larger spark. Both kinds of sparks are caused by opposite charges. Lightning forms in a storm cloud when droplets of water rub against each other as they move up and down in the cloud. The rubbing causes the droplets to develop opposite charges. The droplets with positive charges are lighter, so they move to the top of the cloud. The droplets with negative charges are heavier, so they move to the bottom of the cloud. When this happens, a spark may jump from the negative charges in the bottom of the cloud to the positive charges in the top of the cloud. The spark creates a path for electricity from the bottom to the top of the cloud. The path the electricity follows is the flash of lightning we see.

Lightning can jump from one cloud to another. It can also jump from a cloud to objects on the ground. Tall trees standing alone and tall buildings are more likely to be struck by lightning. The trees and buildings have built up a positive charge. If the bottom of the cloud has a negative charge, lightning may jump from the cloud to the tree or building.

Complete the following using the diagram at the right. The diagram shows lightning jumping from a thundercloud to a lone tree.

1. The negative signs in the bottom of the cloud are   a) protons.   b) electrons.
2. The positive signs on the top of the tree are   a) protons.   b) electrons.
3. The lightning will jump from the cloud to the tree because

   a) the electrical charges are the same.   b) the electrical charges are unlike.

4. In the diagram below, the clouds have electrical charges. Draw lightning symbols that show the lightning jumping from cloud to cloud. Use the symbols to show the direction the lightning would take.

Name: _____ Date: _____

Lightning Rods

We know that it is possible for lightning to strike trees and buildings that have a positive charge. We also know that this is a normal way for atoms to achieve a balanced, neutral charge. However, when lightning strikes a building, the building may be damaged. If a building is made of brick, the spark from the lightning will damage the electrical systems. If a building is made of steel, the heat of the lightning can actually melt parts of the building. And if a building is made of wood, that building can burn down.

How can we avoid these situations? The answer came from Benjamin Franklin. While Franklin is most famous for his kite experiment, he also invented the lightning rod. He realized that lightning was electricity, and that all electricity followed a path. He then concluded that if you gave lightning a path, it would flow to where you wanted it. A lightning rod is a long, pointed rod attached to the top of a building that is connected to the ground with a thick wire. The rod allows electrons to escape slowly, and the wire transfers any static shock from lightning to the ground safely. Because the electrons are channeled, the building is unharmed.

Complete the following.

Write __T__ for true and __F__ for false on the blanks below.

_____ 1. Benjamin Franklin discovered lightning.

_____ 2. Lightning rods channel static electricity into the ground.

_____ 3. Lightning can cause serious damage to buildings and trees.

_____ 4. Lightning rods provide a safe path for electrons to flow to the ground.

_____ 5. Lightning rods attract lightning and are dangerous.

Static Electricity Review

Read each of the following statements. Underline the correct answer.

1. An atom with more protons than electrons has a (positive / negative) charge.

2. An atom with more electrons than protons has a (positive / negative) charge.

3. Atoms do not lose (electrons / protons) by rubbing.

4. Atoms lose (electrons / protons) by rubbing.

Name: _____ Date: _____

5. Two objects with more protons than electrons will (repel / attract) each other.

6. An object with more positively charged protons (+) (repels / attracts) an object with more negatively charged electrons (−).

7. An object with more negatively charged electrons (−) (repels / attracts) an object with more positively charged protons (+).

8. Two objects with more electrons than protons will (repel / attract) each other.

9. On the diagram below, draw a bolt of lightning from the cloud to the objects on the ground where lightning is most likely to strike. Select the objects and draw the lightning bolt. Use the symbol _⌇➤ for lightning. On the blanks below, tell why you have chosen the objects that the lightning bolt struck.

_____

_____

_____

_____

_____

_____

Chapter IX: Electricity

Electrical Currents

As we learned in the previous chapter, static electricity is the movement of electrons from one object to another. The term static tells us that this electricity does not move. While static electricity can be powerful, like lightning, it is not a steady flow. We cannot use it to power our lights, computers, and refrigerators. That requires electricity. **Electricity** is the flow of electrons from one object to another along a conductor. As you recall, most metals are good conductors.

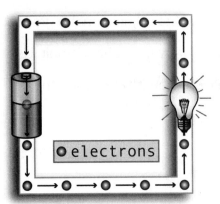

A variety of metals are used to make wires to carry the current of electricity. How can you make electrons move at a steady pace? A generator will produce a steady flow of electricity. Most generators use magnets to push electrons down a wire. This is similar to how a pump would move water out of your basement during a flood. The movement of electrons in a wire produces a current. Again, imagine water flowing out of the pump in your basement. This is similar to how a current of electrons moves down a wire. In a direct current, electrons always move in one direction, from the negative to the positive. To learn more about electrical current, one must know about amperes, volts, watts, and kilowatts.

Amperes, Volts, Watts, and Kilowatts

Amperes, volts, watts, and kilowatts are all ways to measure electricity. Each term deals with a different aspect of the current. **Amperes** measure the number of electrons flowing past a given point in a given period of time. Amp is an abbreviation for amperes. Your cell phone charger may draw 8 amps, which is twice as much as a 4-amp hair dryer.

Voltage is a measure of the speed with which electrons flow past a given point. Voltage is measured in **volts**. In the United States, all outlets deliver 120 volts of electricity. Just about everything we plug in, from hair dryers to refrigerators, is designed to accept the flow of 120 volts. The voltage is higher in Europe, which is why your hair dryer won't work there. So amperes measure the number of electrons, and voltage measures the speed at which they move.

Look around you. Do you see an electrical outlet in your room? When you plug in your hair dryer, it pulls 4 amps. To find out how many watts the hair dryer uses, you multiply the volts by the amps, using the formula **Watts = volts • amperes (I), or W = V • I**. So your hair dryer uses 120 V • 4 I = 480 watts of power. A **watt** measures the amount of energy you consume through the cable. Your cell phone charger uses 120 volts times 8 amps, or 960 watts.

Kilowatts are another way of describing watts. You may recall that *kilo-* means 1,000 in the metric system, and here, a **kilowatt** means 1,000 watts.

Name: _____ Date: _____

Problems Finding Watts

Watts = volts • amps (I)   W = V • I

1. It takes 50 volts to light a bulb. The current flow is 2 amps. Find the watts.

    W = V • I   W = _____ • _____   W = 100

2. It takes 40 volts to light a bulb. The current flow is 1.5 amps. Find the watts.

    W = V • I   W = _____ • _____   W = _____

3. It takes 120 volts to power a toaster. The current flow is 5 amps.

    Find the watts.

    W = V • I   W = _____ • _____   W = _____

4. It takes 120 volts to run a microwave. The current flow is 8 amps. Find the watts.

    W = V • I   W = _____ • _____   W = _____

Problems Finding Kilowatts

1. It takes 120 volts to power a computer. The computer draws 15 amps.

    Find the watts and kilowatts.

    W = V • I   W = _____ • _____   W = _____

                             KW = _____

2. It takes 120 volts to power a freezer. The freezer draws 22 amps. Find the watts and

    kilowatts.

    W = V • I   W = _____ • _____   W = _____   KW = _____

3. It takes 120 volts to power a washer. The washer draws 33 amps. Find the watts and

    kilowatts.

    W = V • I   W = _____ • _____   W = _____   KW = _____

4. It takes 120 volts to power a furnace. The heater draws 45 amps. Find the watts and

    kilowatts.

    W = V • I   W = _____ • _____   W = _____   KW = _____

Name: _____ Date: _____

Watt-hours

It is good to know about amps, volts, and watts, but one of the most important ways to describe electricity is watt-hours and kilowatt-hours. Watt-hours and kilowatt-hours are used to tell how much electric power has been used. This is the way the electric company measures how much energy you use and, based on those totals, decides how much to bill you. One watt used for one hour is one **watt-hour**. The number of watt-hours is found by multiplying the watts used by the number of hours.

> *Example:* A 75-watt light bulb is used for 2 hours. To find the watts used, multiply watts times hours. 75 watts times 2 hours = 150 watt-hours.

Find the watt-hours.

1. A lamp with a 100-watt bulb is used for 2 hours.

    _____ watts • _____ hours = _____ watt-hours

2. A lamp with a 40-watt bulb is used for 4 hours.

    _____ w • _____ hrs. = _____ watt-hours

3. A lamp with a 75-watt bulb is used for 10 hours.

    _____ w • _____ hrs. = _____ watt-hours

4. A lamp with a 100-watt bulb is used for 10 hours.

    _____ w • _____ hrs. = _____ watt-hours

Kilowatt-hours

One thousand watt-hours equals one kilowatt-hour.

> *Example:* A 40-watt bulb used for 25 hours equals 1,000 watt-hours. 1,000 watt-hours equals 1 kilowatt-hour.

Find the kilowatt-hours.

1. A 200-watt bulb must be on   a) 1   b) 3   c) 5   d) 7   hours to equal
    1 kilowatt-hour.

2. A 50-watt bulb must be on   a) 10   b) 20   c) 30   d) 40   hours to equal
    1 kilowatt-hour.

3. A 100-watt bulb must be on   a) 10   b) 20   c) 30   d) 40   hours to equal
    1 kilowatt-hour.

4. A 200-watt bulb must be on   a) 2   b) 4   c) 8   d) 10   hours to equal
    2 kilowatt-hours.

Name: _____ Date: _____

Solve the following.

5. A toaster using 400 watts per hour will equal 1 kilowatt-hour in

   a) 1   b) $1\frac{1}{2}$ c) 2   d) $2\frac{1}{2}$ hours.

6. A television using 500 watts per hour will equal 2 kilowatt-hours in

   a) 2   b) 4   c) 6   d) 8   hours.

7. A refrigerator uses 1 kilowatt-hour per day. The refrigerator is using

   a) 1,000   b) 2,000   c) 3,000   d) 4,000   watt-hours per day.

8. A clothes dryer uses 3 kilowatt-hours per month. The clothes dryer is using

   a) 1,000   b) 2,000   c) 3,000   d) 4,000

   watt-hours per month.

Say the electric company charges you 10 cents per kilowatt-hour of electricity you use. How much would it cost for you to …

9. Run a 10,000-watt air conditioner for 13 hours (total) a day for 30 days? _____

10. Run a 300-watt ceiling fan for 13 hours (total) a day for 30 days? _____

11. Run a 100-watt light bulb for 5 hours (total) a day for 30 days? _____

12. Run a 480-watt hair dryer for 30 minutes (total) a day for 30 days? _____

Name: _____ Date: _____

Resistance

Now that you understand amperes, volts, and watts, there is one more thing you need to know about electricity. Remember how we learned that some materials, such as plastic, do not conduct electricity very well, while other materials, such as metal, conduct electricity easily? Copper is a metal that is a very good conductor. Electrons move freely through copper and create a current. **Resistance** is how much something tries to slow down the flow of electrons through it. There is a resistance to the flow of electrons through different kinds of wire.

Resistance was identified by a scientist named Georg Ohm. Ohm wanted to find the strength of electric currents. He found that the circumference of the wire, the length of the wire, and the metal the wire is made of can be used to find the strength of the current. The larger the wire circumference, which is also known as the gauge of the wire, the more easily the electrons flow. The shorter the wire, the less resistance to the wire. A copper wire resists the flow of electrons less than many other metals. A long copper wire resists the flow more than does a short wire. A thin copper wire resists the flow more than a thick wire.

Think of it like a water pipe. It is more difficult to move water through a long, narrow pipe than a short, narrow pipe. It is more difficult to move water through a short, narrow pipe than it is through a short, wide pipe. The long, narrow pipe provides the most resistance to water. It is the same for electrons moving through a wire.

Material also plays an important role. As we mentioned earlier, copper is a highly conductive metal. Electrons will move more easily down a copper wire than a lead wire. Electrons will move down a lead wire more easily than they would a cloth string.

Answer the following.

1. You have two copper wires. They are both the same length. Wire "A" has a circumference twice that of Wire "B." The strength of electricity will be greater in

    a) Wire "A."   b) Wire "B."

2. You have two copper wires. They are both the same circumference. Wire "A" has a length of 6 feet. Wire "B" has a length of 12 feet. The strength of current will be greater in

    a) Wire "A."   b) Wire "B."

3. You have two wires. They are both the same circumference and the same length. Wire "A" is made of steel. Wire "B" is made of copper. The current will flow more strongly in

    a) Wire "A."   b) Wire "B."

Name: _____ Date: _____

4. Place a plus sign (+) on the blank for the wire that has the greater resistance to the flow of electricity.

circumference 1"

circumference 3"

_____ A. Copper wire, length 12 inches   _____ B. Copper wire, length 12 inches

5. Place a plus sign (+) on the blank for the wire that would have the greater resistance. Each wire has the same circumference. The lengths of the wires are not the same.

circumference 1"

circumference 1"

_____ A.   _____ B.

Ohm's Law

Ohm devised a formula to identify the level of resistance a conductor has. Known as **Ohm's Law**, the law states that voltage divided by current tell us how much the circuit resists the flow. The formula for Ohm's Law is **Resistance Ω = Volts ÷ I (amps)**, which is written as **R Ω = V ÷ I.**

Find the resistance.

1. A 1.5-volt battery is used to light a small bulb. The amps (I) are 0.3.

   R Ω = V ÷ I   R Ω = _____ ÷ _____   R Ω = _____

2. Two 1.5-volt batteries are needed for a flashlight.

   The two 1.5-volt batteries equal 3.0 volts. The amps (I) are 0.3.

   R Ω = V ÷ I   R Ω = _____ ÷ _____   R Ω = _____

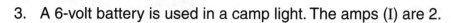

3. A 6-volt battery is used in a camp light. The amps (I) are 2.

   R Ω = V ÷ I   R Ω = _____ ÷ _____   R Ω = _____

4. A 12-volt battery is used to run a small motor. The amps (I) are 2.

   R Ω = V ÷ I   R Ω = _____ ÷ _____   R Ω = _____

Name: _____ Date: _____

Now that we know how to figure out the resistance, we can use that formula rearranged to identify the amperes and voltage.

Problems Finding Amperes

The amperes can be found using the formula: **amps (I) = volts ÷ resistance I = V ÷ R Ω**

1. A light in a circuit resists the flow by 30 ohms (Ω). A 6-volt battery is used to make the light

   glow. Find the amps: I = V ÷ R Ω   I = _____ ÷ _____   I = _____ amps

2. A 3.0-volt battery is used in an electric circuit. A light in the circuit resists the current flow

   by 15 Ω. Find the amps: I = V ÷ R Ω   I = _____ ÷ _____   I = _____ amps

3. A light resists the current flow by 24 Ω. A 12-volt battery is used to make the light glow.

   Find the amps: I = V ÷ R Ω   I = _____ ÷ _____   I = _____ amps

4. A 4.5-volt battery is used in an electrical circuit. A light in the circuit resists at 15 Ω.

   Find the amps: I = V ÷ R Ω   I = _____ ÷ _____   I = _____ amps

Problems Finding Voltage

Volts may be found using: **Voltage = I (amperes) • Resistance   V = I • R Ω**

1. A battery is used for a light. The current flow is 0.20 amps. The current flow is resisted by

   30 Ω. Volts = _____ I • _____ Ω   Volts = _____

2. A battery is used for a fan. The current flow is 2 amps.

   The current flow is resisted by 2 Ω.

   Volts = _____ I • _____ Ω   Volts = _____

3. A light is used for reading. The current flow is 30 amps.

   The current flow is resisted by 4 Ω.

   Volts = _____ I • _____ Ω   V = _____

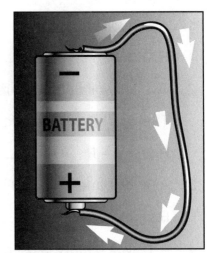

4. A toy truck is run by a battery. The current flow is 0.5 amps.

   The current flow is resisted by 3 Ω.

   Volts = _____ I • _____ Ω   V = _____

Name: _____ Date: _____

Circuits

   Let's look at electricity in action. The easiest way to see how the flow of electrons works is to look at the lightbulb. By itself, the lightbulb doesn't do much. But connect it to a battery with a copper wire to carry the electrons, and you have an electrical circuit.

   Batteries have two terminals, or ends. One is positive, one is negative, and electrons move from the negative terminal to the positive terminal. The copper wire must connect to both terminals to complete the circuit. You may then add a load, the lightbulb. The electrons, which were zipping around the wire, now must pass through the lightbulb.

   How does the lightbulb actually light up? To understand that, we must think back to Ohm and his Law. The electrons move into the lightbulb at a rate of speed similar to their speed in the copper wire. Then they run into the thin filament of the lightbulb. The electrons encounter greater resistance from the filament, and they are forced to slow down. It's hard work to slow the flow of electrons down, and the filament heats up in the process, causing it to glow. The filament doesn't stop the electrons; they continue back out of the lightbulb and through the wire, to the positive terminal of the battery. This is a complete simple circuit.

Note: In all the circuit diagrams, the arrows show the direction of the **flow of electrons** from the negative battery terminal to the positive battery terminal.

Answer the following.

1. Complete the following for the electric circuit. Write the following in the correct rectangles below.

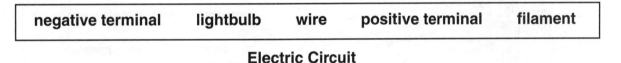

negative terminal	lightbulb	wire	positive terminal	filament

Electric Circuit

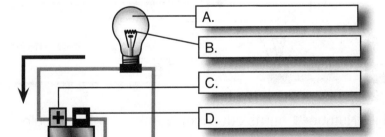

A.

B.

C.

D.

E.

Answer the following about the circuit diagram above.

2. The filament (conducts / resists) the flow of current.

3. The source of the flow of current in the circuit is (the lightbulb / the battery).

4. The electrons flow from the (positive / negative) post of the battery through the circuit.

Name: _____ Date: _____

Series and Parallel Circuits

Lights Wired in Series

What happens when you increase the load on a circuit? When two lightbulbs are wired in **series**, both lights are on the same copper wire. If one light burns out, then the circuit is broken. The current cannot flow, so both lights go out, even though one light has not burned out. This is what happened on old-fashioned Christmas tree lights. If one light was bad, the whole strand went dark, and some unlucky person had to try all the bulbs to find which one was burnt out.

Again, think back to Ohm's Law. What do you think has happened to the resistance level when we added a second lightbulb to the circuit? The second lightbulb added a load to the circuit. The second lightbulb added more resistance to the flow of current. If you place more lightbulbs, or loads, on a circuit, you increase the resistance to the flow of electrons through the circuit.

Label the diagram.

The following diagram shows two lights in an electrical circuit wired in series. Place the following in the rectangle by the correct letter.

lightbulb   negative terminal   filament   copper wire   positive terminal

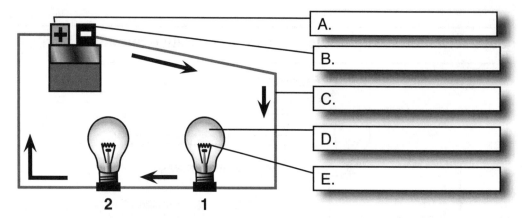

A.

B.

C.

D.

E.

2   1

1. The filament in Light Number 1 burns out. Light Number 2 will   a) glow.   b) not glow.

2. The filament in Light Number 2 burns out. Light Number 1 will   a) glow.   b) not glow.

3. Some Christmas tree lights are wired in series. This means that if

    a) one light goes out, all the lights go out.

    b) one light goes out, the other lights will not go out.

4. When lights are wired in series, there is (one / more than one) path for the current.

5. The amount of resistance to the flow of current (increases / decreases) as more loads are added to a circuit.

Name: _____ Date: _____

Lights Wired in Parallel

These day, the newer Christmas tree lights are wired in parallel. Each lightbulb is on a single circuit that is separate from all the other bulbs. This is good news for that unlucky person who usually gets stuck testing lightbulbs every year. Since every lightbulb is on its own circuit, there is no increase in resistance to the flow of current.

Label the diagram.

The following diagram shows two lights in an electrical circuit wired in parallel. Place the following in the rectangle by the correct letter.

battery	lightbulbs	copper wire	flow of electrons

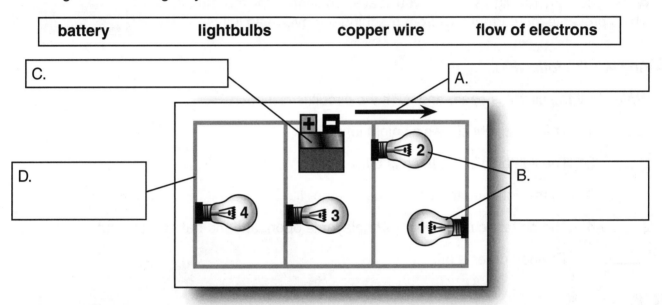

Underline the correct answer.

1. The filament in Light Number 1 burns out. Lights Number 2, 3, and 4 will

    a) glow.   b) not glow.

2. The filament in Light Number 2 burns out. Lights Number 1, 3, and 4 will

    a) glow.   b) not glow.

3. The filament in Light Number 3 burns out. Lights Number 1, 2, and 4 will

    a) glow.   b) not glow.

4. The filament in Light Number 4 burns out. Lights Number 1, 2, and 3 will

    a) glow.   b) not glow.

5. When lights are wired in a parallel circuit there is   a) one   b) more than one

    path for the current.

6. Some Christmas tree lights are wired in a parallel circuit. This means that if

    a) one light goes out, all the lights go out.

    b) one light goes out, the other lights will not go out.

85

Name: _____ Date: _____

Switches

     We talked about breaking a circuit, but did you know you break circuits all the time? Every time you turn something that uses electricity on or off, you are completing and interrupting a circuit. A **switch** is a device that controls the current flow. When a switch is connected, or **closed**, the current flows, completing the circuit as it moves through the load. In other words, when you flip the light switch on in the kitchen, you are completing the circuit and allowing the electrons to move through the load, the overhead lights. When the switch is disconnected, or **open**, you are breaking the circuit, preventing the electrons from moving. When you turn the lights off as you leave, you interrupt the circuit, which prevents the current flow from reaching the overhead lights.

Answer the following.

Write "O" if the circuit is open, and "C" if the circuit is closed.

_____ 1. The night light shines all night long.

_____ 2. The lightbulb in the lamp is burned out.

_____ 3. All the lights on the Christmas tree are lit.

_____ 4. The battery case to your MP3 player is open, and the battery falls out.

_____ 5. The hair dryer is off.

Name: _____ Date: _____

Chapter X: Light Refraction and Reflection

Light

What do you think of when you think of light? You may think of the sun, the lightbulb in your room, or a candle. Our main source of light energy is the sun. Sunlight is white light that travels to Earth in straight lines. The white light is comprised of the visible colors of the electromagnetic spectrum. When light hits an object, two possible things that can happen are reflection and refraction.

Reflected Light

Rays from white light from the sun may be reflected. When rays of light travel through the air, they travel in a straight line. When a light ray strikes a rough surface, such as sand, it scatters. Sand has no reflection, which means you can't see your face in it. When light rays strike a shiny object, they bounce off. The bouncing of light rays off a surface is called **reflection**. A mirror is a shiny object, and the light rays bouncing off its shiny surface are what we see.

Angle of Incidence and Angle of Reflection

As we already mentioned, light rays travel in straight lines. When a light ray hits a shiny object, like the mirror, it does not scatter. The light ray is reflected. The angle that the incoming ray makes with the perpendicular line, called the normal, is the **angle of incidence**. The angle the reflected ray makes with the normal is called the **angle of reflection**. The angle of reflection equals the angle of incidence. When an incoming light ray "I" strikes the shiny mirror below at point "x," the light ray "I" is reflected back along the path "R." The angle at which the ray is reflected equals the angle of incidence. In other words, the reflected light ray is reflected at the same angle, but in the opposite direction.

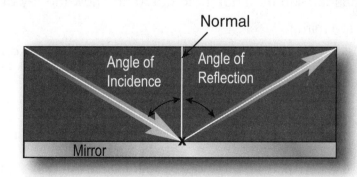

Name: _____   Date: _____

Using the Protractor to Measure Angles of Incidence

In angles A and B below, a protractor is used to measure the angles. Note how the protractor must be placed on the normal line to measure the angles.

Complete the following.

Angle A

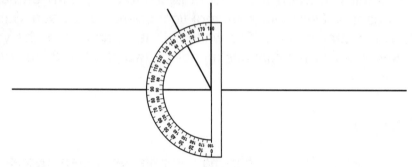

1. The measure of Angle A above is _____ degrees.

Angle B

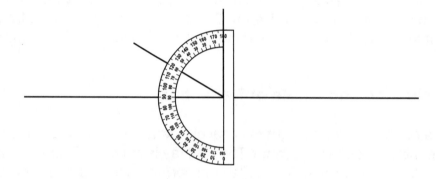

2. The measure of Angle B above is _____ degrees.

3. In the diagram below, draw over the dashed line from dot "a" to dot "b" to show the ray of light hitting the mirror.

4. The angle between the light ray and the normal is   a) 90   b) 10   c) 40   d) 80   degrees.

5. Draw over the dashed line from dot "b" to dot "c" to show the ray of light bouncing off, or reflecting, from the mirror.

6. The angle between the reflected light ray and the normal is   a) 90   b) 40   c) 10   d) 80   degrees.

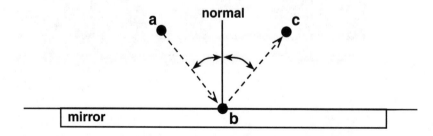

Name: _____ Date: _____

Determining the Angle of Reflection

When a light ray strikes an object, like a mirror, and is reflected, the angle of reflection will be the same as the angle between the light ray and the normal line.

1. Diagram A below shows a light ray striking an object. Draw over the dashed line to show the angle of reflection.

Diagram A

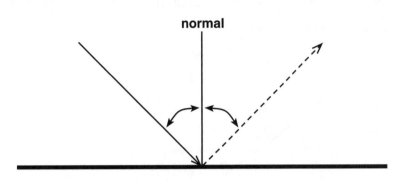

2. The angle that the incoming light ray makes with the normal line in Diagram A is 45 degrees. The angle of reflection will be   a) 90   b) 45   c) 60   d) 10   degrees.

Measuring the Angle of Reflection

Use your protractor to measure the angle of incidence. Then, measure the angle of reflection as the light bounces off the surface. Write your answer in the appropriate blanks.

1.

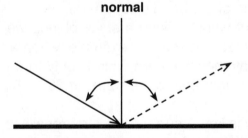

Angle of Incidence: _____

Angle of Reflection: _____

2.

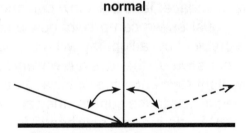

Angle of Incidence: _____

Angle of Reflection: _____

3.

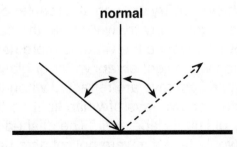

Angle of Incidence: _____

Angle of Reflection: _____

Name: _____ Date: _____

Answer the following. (A protractor will be needed for this exercise.)

4. The angle of incidence in the diagram below is   a) 25   b) 35   c) 45   d) 55
   degrees.

5. The angle of reflection in the diagram below is   a) 25   b) 35   c) 45   d) 55
   degrees.

6. The angle of incidence and angle of reflection from a smooth surface are
   (equal / unequal) angles.

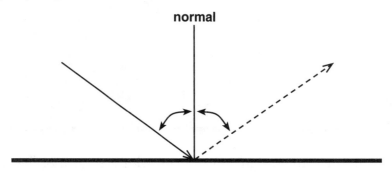

Refracted Light Rays

Refracted light rays are light rays that are bent. When light goes from one medium to another, it may bend due to the different densities of the mediums. For example, as light goes from air through glass and water, it slows down and bends. How can you tell? If you fill a glass of water and put a straw in it, you will notice that the straw looks as though it bends at the water's surface. Take the straw out, and the appearance of the bend disappears.

Just as we can predict how a light ray will react when striking a shiny object, we can also predict how a light ray will react when it enters water or glass. For example, when a light ray enters water, the rays are **refracted**, which is to say they are **bent**. This is only true if the white light rays enter the water at an angle. If the white light enters the water at 90°, which is perpendicular to the surface, they are not refracted.

Why do the light rays bend? Remember, density is key. A surface like a mirror will reflect the light rays. A mirror is too dense for the light ray to penetrate. A surface like a brick will scatter a light ray. It is also too dense for the light rays to penetrate. Water is not as dense as mirrors or bricks. So light rays are able to penetrate water. However, water is more dense than air, so the light rays are slowed down.

It's the same thing that happens when you enter the water. Try walking at a regular pace on the sidewalk. You move along at a steady, even pace, right? Now try walking at the same pace in a pool. It's much harder and you move much slower because the water is more dense than the air. The same thing happens with light rays. When white light enters water or glass at an angle, the white rays of light are slowed down. The white light rays are refracted when they leave the air and enter water or glass. The diagram below shows rays of white light as they strike the surface of water at an angle. The incoming ray of light is labeled "I." The dashed line "N" is a line for normal. Normal is the path the light ray would take if it were not refracted as it enters the water. The letter "R" is the refracted ray of light after it enters the water.

Name: _____ Date: _____

Using the diagram, answer the following questions.

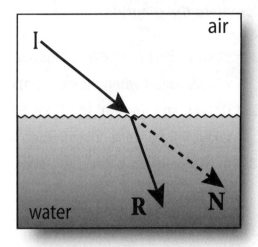

1. Water is (more dense / less dense) than air.

2. When the ray of light "I" enters the water, it is (reflected / refracted).

3. When the ray of light "I" enters the water, it is refracted (away from / toward) normal.

4. The arrow showing the refracted ray of light is (arrow N / arrow R).

In the diagram below, a light source is below the water level. The light moves from water to air. The refracted ray is "R," and the normal is marked "N."

Use the below diagram and answer the questions that follow.

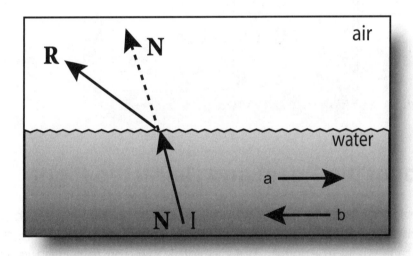

5. Air is (less dense / more dense) than water.

6. When the ray "I" leaves the water and enters the air, it is refracted (toward / away from) normal.

7. The arrow showing the refracted light is (arrow R / arrow N).

8. When a ray of light moves from water and enters air that is less dense, the light is refracted (away from normal / toward normal).

9. When a ray of light moves from less dense air to water that is more dense, the light ray is refracted (away from normal / toward normal).

Name: _____ Date: _____

Complete the diagram.

1. Draw a line from "a" to "b" for each ray of light. This is the path the rays of light take as they are refracted when they enter the water.

2. Draw a line from "a" to "d" for each ray of light. This is the path the light rays would have taken if they were not refracted when they entered the water.

3. In the diagram below, you think the fish are at "b." Shade in the ellipses at "d" to show where the fish are really located.

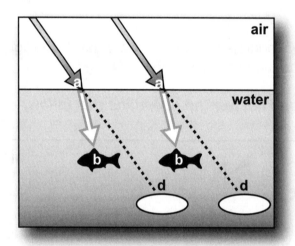

Learning About the Prism and Refracted Light

As we have learned, white light rays are refracted, or bent, when they pass through objects with different densities. This makes it seem like straws are broken and fish are in one place when they are actually in another. But did you know that refraction is also how we get rainbows?

Sunlight comes from the sun as rays of white of light. However, each ray of white light is made up of different wavelengths of light. How can this be? Think back to when you finger-painted as a child. If you mixed up all the colors together, you were left with a puddle of black goop. When you mix colors, they all combine to form the color black. That's what happens with white light rays, only all the wavelengths combine to make white. Just remember, light and color are not the same thing. Colors combine to form black, while light wavelengths combine to form white. When we see each of these wavelengths, we see colors, but more about that later.

A prism can be used to see the many colors in a ray of white light. When a ray of white light enters a prism, the white light is slowed down. The slowing down of the white light as it leaves the air and enters the glass prism causes the white light to be refracted. When this happens, the different wavelengths that make up the light bend at different angles. When the

Name: _____ Date: _____

refracted white light leaves the prism, we can see the red, orange, yellow, green, blue, indigo, and violet colors. It is refracted (bent) light that produces rainbows.

The diagram below shows a ray of white light entering the prism. The ray of white light is refracted as it enters the prism. Then the refracted light can be seen as the different colors of visible light.

Color the diagram.

1. Color each arrow of refracted light using g. red, f. orange, e. yellow, d. green, c. blue, b. indigo, and a. violet.

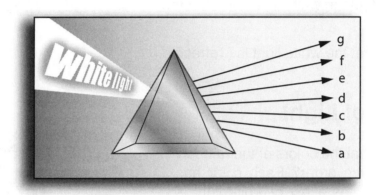

When the white light enters the prism, it is separated into the colors that can be seen by the human eye. Each of the colors has a different wavelength. Each wavelength is refracted (bent) a different amount as it enters the prism. When the white light enters the prism and breaks up into the many wavelengths of colored light, it has a special name. The name is **dispersion**. The white light is dispersed into red, orange, yellow, green, blue, indigo, and violet light.

Refracted and Reflected Light and Rainbows

The diagram on the next page represents a spherical droplet of water in the atmosphere. The white light from the sun enters the droplet of water and is refracted. This bending changes the angle of the white light. Then the ray of light is reflected off the back of the droplet. When the ray leaves the droplet, it is refracted again. How does that make a rainbow? Each time the ray is refracted, the different wavelengths bend at a slightly different angle. That angle is no longer parallel, and increases over distance. By the time the wavelengths reach our eyes, they have spread out enough to be visible in the rainbow.

It's important to remember that three things must occur for you to see a rainbow. There

must be small sphere-shaped droplets of water floating in the air. The sun must be behind you, and the droplets must be in front of you. If all of these conditions are met, you will see the beautiful colors of the rainbow.

Name: _____ Date: _____

Complete the following.

1. Draw over line "a" to show the white light from the sun that is entering the droplet of water.

2. Draw over line "b" to show the bent, or refracted, light as it enters the droplet of water and hits the opposite side of the droplet.

3. Draw over line "c" to show the reflected light as it bounces off the droplet of water.

4. Line "b" shows that the white light is (refracted / reflected).

5. Line "c" shows that the white light is (refracted / reflected).

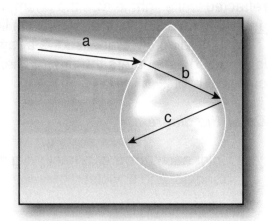

Wavelengths of Light

Did you know that the colors of the rainbow are always in the same order? Each color has a different wavelength. As a ray of white light is dispersed, each color's wavelength bends at a slightly different angle. Red has the longest wavelength. Violet has the shortest wavelength. Each color's wavelength never changes, so the order in which we see the colors never changes.

The long and short wavelengths in the white light ray make up the primary and secondary colors. The human eye can see these colors. The visible colors (primary and secondary colors) are red, orange, yellow, green, blue, indigo, and violet. Each of the visible colors has its own wavelength and wave frequency. The wave frequency is the number of waves that passes a point in a given time.

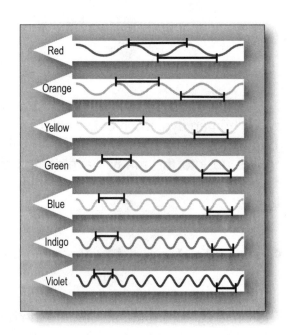

Use the picture to answer the following.

1. The color with the longest wavelength is   a) yellow.   b) orange.   c) red.

2. The color with the shortest wavelength is   a) blue.   b) violet.   c) indigo.

3. We can see primary and secondary colors because each color has a different (amplitude / wavelength).

4. Each of the primary and secondary colors has its own _____ and

   _____ .

Name: _____ Date: _____

We know that the order of the colors in a rainbow never changes. The way to remember the order of the colors is to remember the name ROY G. BIV. That stands for:

R = Red
O = Orange
Y = Yellow
G = Green
B = Blue
I = Indigo
V = Violet

Complete the diagram.

5. On the diagram there are lettered blanks. For each lettered blank, write in the color below that has the same letter as the blank. Then color the rainbow.

    a. violet
    b. indigo
    c. blue
    d. green
    e. yellow
    f. orange
    g. red

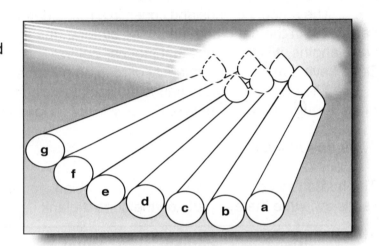

Identify the terms related to rainbows and prisms.

Place the letter "P" on the blank if the term is related to a prism. Place the letter "R" if the term is related to a rainbow. Place both the letters "P" and "R" on the blank if it relates to both a prism and a rainbow.

_____ 1. spherical droplets of water

_____ 2. semicircle in shape

_____ 3. visible colors of light appear

_____ 4. white light rays from sun are refracted

_____ 5. reflected rays from droplets of water

_____ 6. refracted rays result in primary and secondary colors

_____ 7. parallel white light rays

_____ 8. visible colors of light come from a man-made object

Name: _____ Date: _____

How Does the Human Eye See Color?

We see colors everywhere. But how do our brains know what color we are seeing? The answer is that our eyes process the information for us. When we look at a shiny blue car, light is reflecting off the surface. The car is absorbing the wavelengths of all the colors except blue. The blue wavelength is reflected back to us. Some of that light is entering our eyes through the **cornea**, the convex lens that is the exterior shape of the eye. The light then moves through the **pupil**, which is the dark spot at the center of the iris. The **iris** is the colored part of the eye. The pupil widens if there is not a lot of light available, or narrows if it is really bright out. The light is then refracted through the **lens** onto the back of the eye, where the retina is. The **retina** is made up of light-sensitive tissue called **rods** and **cones**.

The amount of rods and cones in a retina determines how much color you see. The rods see better in the dark, and the cones better in the light. Since color is light reflecting different wavelengths, it is the cones that process colors. This is why dogs do not see colors like we do. Dogs have a much larger quantity of rods, to help them hunt at night.

The rods and cones change the light particles to electrical signals, which are sent to the brain through the **optic nerve**. There, your brain identifies what it is you are seeing.

Fill in the blanks.

The human eye diagram has a letter with a blank for each of the following eye parts. Using the list below, write the eye parts on the correct blank.

iris	**cornea**	**pupil**	**lens**	**retina**
optic nerve		**rods and cones**		

a. _____

b. _____

c. _____

d. _____

e. _____

f. _____

g. _____ _____

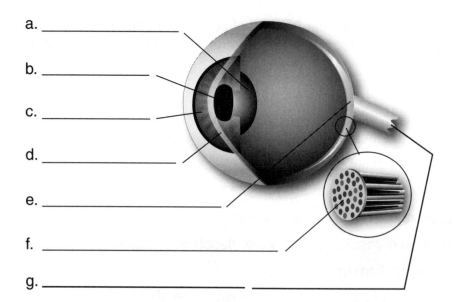

Name: _____ Date: _____

White light rays may be reflected, absorbed, or transmitted. When a white light ray strikes an object, some of the visible light may be reflected. The object may absorb some of

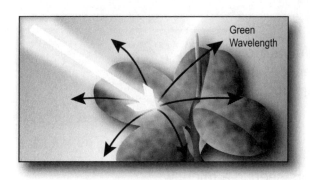

the visible rays. Certain colors are absorbed and others are reflected. It is the reflected light rays that can be seen as color in an object. Each of the light ray colors has its own frequency. When an object reflects a color, our eyes see the object as that color. When you see a green leaf, the leaf is not green. The green wavelength of visible light is being reflected. The green leaf has absorbed the other colors in the white light. You do not see the absorbed colors.

The atmosphere is loaded with tiny particles. These particles are important in the colors we see in the sky. When white light hits the particles, some light waves of color are scattered. Some wavelengths of color are scattered more than others. The blues and violets are scattered most. So we see a blue sky.

Read each of the statements and select the correct answer.

1. There is a red tulip. The visible light wave being reflected is

    a) blue.   b) red.   c) green.   d) yellow.

2. A large plant has yellow petals. The visible light wave being reflected is

    a) blue.   b) red.   c) green.   d) yellow.

3. A friend has a very nice blue shirt. The visible light wave being reflected is

    a) blue.   b) red.   c) green.   d) yellow.

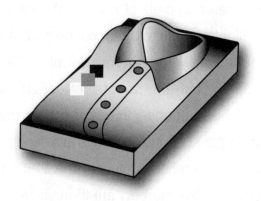

Name: _____ Date: _____

Reviewing Refracted and Reflected Light

Complete the paragraphs.

The selection below has blanks where a meaningful part of the sentence has been left out. Above each selection are numbered statements. Select the numbered statement that completes each sentence and write it in the blank.

1. The slowing down of the white light as it leaves the air
2. up of wavelengths that make up the many colors seen in a rainbow
3. A prism can be used to help you understand
4. be refracted into the many different wavelengths that make up the colors in a rainbow
5. act much like a prism

     Normally, we see white light as it passes through air. However, each ray of white light is made _____. When a ray of white light enters a prism, the white light is slowed down. _____ and enters the prism causes the white light to _____. When the refracted white light leaves a prism, we can see the beautiful red, orange, yellow, green, blue, indigo, and violet colors. In the sky, the small spherical droplets of water _____. Rainbows develop because as the ray of white light enters the spherical droplet, the speed of the white light is slowed down and refracted.

6. spherical droplets of water
7. water is spherical
8. bent, or refracted
9. parallel rays of white light
10. or refracted

     Light comes from the sun as _____. Rainbows are possible when the parallel rays of sunlight enter droplets of water in the atmosphere. The shape of the droplets of _____. When the sunlight enters the spherical droplet of water, the ray of light is _____. The ray of light then hits the inside wall of the droplet of water, and it is bounced, or reflected, to another part of the droplet. Then the ray of light departs, or leaves, the spherical droplet and is again bent. Imagine this happening in a sky that has many small _____. The droplets are all receiving light rays from the sun. The light rays are bent, _____, as they enter the droplets, then the light rays bounce, or are reflected. Finally the light rays depart from the droplets and are refracted again. The colors of the rainbow are then visible.

Name: _____ Date: _____

Chapter XI: Understanding Waves

Waves

What do you think of when you think of waves? Most people will think of waves on water. Perhaps you thought of the wavelengths of light from the previous chapter. Did you also know that sound travels in waves? There are many kinds of waves. There are light waves, sound waves, and electric waves. Some waves cannot be seen with the eye, like sound waves, while others, like waves on water, can be seen. All waves are alike in many ways.

Speed of Light and Sound Waves

We have already discussed how light waves can reflect or refract as they move through different mediums. Air and water are known as **mediums** through which waves move. As we already know, the speed of the waves is a result of how dense the medium is. Light waves traveling from the medium of air through the medium of water will bend, or refract. Sound waves are also slowed down as they travel through a different medium. Think back to the last time you went swimming. Perhaps your friend tried to get your attention underwater and shouted. You heard the shout, but you couldn't understand the words. That's because the waves were slowed down by the density of the water.

The temperature of the medium is also important to how waves travel. Have you ever noticed how much louder things seem in the summer? That's because warm air is less dense than cold air, and waves travel faster through less dense mediums. As a result, traffic, sirens, and your little sister's screams all seem louder in the summer.

While light wavelengths and sound waves may act much alike as they pass through different mediums, they are moving at different speeds. Sound waves travel at about 1,100 feet per second, or 334 meters per second, in air. Light waves travel at 186,000 miles per second in air. That's why, when you are watching the fireworks show on the Fourth of July, you always see the illumination of the fireworks long before you hear the explosion.

Name: _____ Date: _____

Speed of Sound Waves

You can tell how far away a storm is by counting the seconds between the time you see lightning and hear thunder. How far away is each storm below?

Solve the following.

Sound travels about 1,100 feet per second in air. There are 5,280 feet in a mile.

1. You see lightning and 5 seconds later hear thunder.
   The storm is about   a) 1   b) 2   c) 3   d) 4
   mile(s) from you.
2. You see lightning and 10 seconds later hear thunder.
   The storm is (more than / less than) 2 miles from you.

Solve the following.

Sound travels about 334 meters per second in air.
There are 1,336 meters in a mile.

3. You see lightning and 3 seconds later hear thunder.
   The storm is about   a) 100   b) 1,000   c) 2,000   d) 3,000 meters from you.
4. You see lightning and 6 seconds later hear thunder. The storm is about (2,000 / 3,000) meters from you.

Speed of Light Waves

Solve the following.

Light waves travel at a speed of 186,000 miles per second.

1. Assume the Earth is in its orbit 90,000,000 miles from the sun. It takes a light ray about
   a) 2   b) 4   c) 6   d) 8   seconds to travel from the sun to the earth.
2. Assume Mercury is in its orbit 40,000,000 miles from the sun. It takes a light ray from the sun about   a) 3.6   b) 4.6   c) 5.6   d) 6.6   seconds to travel from the sun to Mercury.

Name: _____ Date: _____

Understanding How Waves Are Alike

All waves have wavelength, amplitude, and frequency. The highest point on all waves is called the **crest**, and the lowest point is called the **trough**. When you are measuring the **wavelength**, you are measuring the distance from one crest to the next, or one trough to the next. To find the **amplitude**, you have to find the center and then measure the displacement of a crest or trough from that center. **Frequency** is a measurement of how many waves are completed in a specific period of time. For example, one wave per second has a frequency of one hertz. The following diagrams will help you understand how light waves, sound waves, radio waves, and water waves are alike.

Complete the following.

1. Connect a-b with a line on Diagram A to show a wavelength, which is from one high point to the next high point. Label a-b "crest."
2. Connect c-d with a line to show a wavelength, which is from one low point to the next low point. Label c-d "trough." A wavelength is crest to crest or trough to trough.
3. Connect e-f with a line to show the amplitude, which is the distance from the baseline to the crest or trough.
    Diagram A

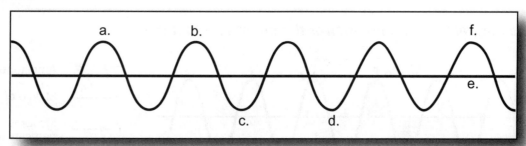

4. Connect g-h with a line on Diagram B to show a wavelength, which is from one high point to the next high point. Label g-h "crest."
5. Connect i-j with a line to show a wavelength, which is from one low point to the next low point. Label i-j "trough." A wavelength is crest to crest or trough to trough.
6. Connect k-l with a line to show the amplitude, which is the distance from the baseline to the crest or trough. Another word for amplitude is displacement.
    Diagram B

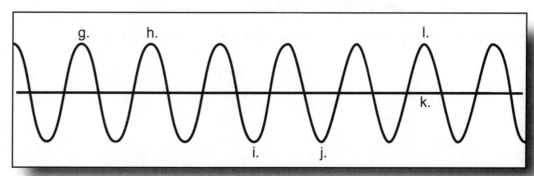

Name: _____ Date: _____

How Waves Work

Waves work because of vibrations. Vibrations are the repeated motion of things—sound, light, water—moving along a path. These waves may move in two directions. Some waves move longitudinally. Longitudinal waves move from side to side, in the same direction the vibrations move. Sound waves move longitudinally. Transverse waves move up and down, perpendicular to the vibrations. Light waves are examples of transverse waves. Some waves move both longitudinally and transversely. Waves over the surface of water move up and down, but also they move a little bit forward, which gives these waves a circular appearance as they move over the water.

Longitudinal Waves

In a longitudinal wave, an object moves from side to side in the wave. What does that mean? Let's say your mother yells for you to come to dinner. When she yells, the force of her voice pushes the air in waves. The air moves in the same direction the wave moves, all the way upstairs. The waves are moving side to side, and the air is being pushed from side to side. It takes a lot of energy to move the waves through the air over a long distance, and finally, the waves begin to slow down and spread out. This is why your mom's yelling isn't as loud upstairs as it is in the kitchen. The waves have slowed down.

Use the diagram below and answer the questions that follow.

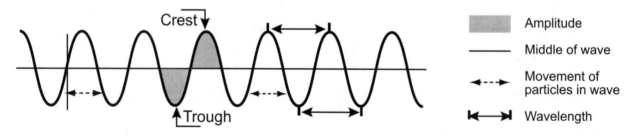

1. The high point of the wave is the (trough / crest).

2. The low point of the wave is the (trough / crest).

3. The amplitude of the wave is the distance from the middle of the wave to the top of the

   _____ and bottom of the _____.

4. In this wave, an object in the wave moves (side to side / up and down).

Name: _____ Date: _____

Transverse Waves

In transverse waves, an object in the wave moves up and down. Picture it like this. Your dad asks you to water the grass. So you get the hose, turn it on, and nothing happens. There is a kink in the hose about 15 feet behind you. So you begin to make a wave with the hose to knock the kink free. The up and down motion of your hand is transported down the hose by traversal waves until it hits the kink. You manage to knock the kink lose, but that absorbed all the energy of the wave, so the wave stops.

Use the diagram below, and answer the questions that follow.

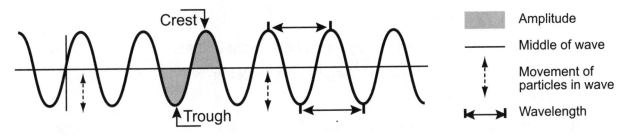

1. The high point of a transverse wave is the (trough / crest).

2. The low point of a transverse wave is the (trough / crest).

3. The amplitude of a transverse wave is the distance from the middle of the wave to the top

   of the _____ and bottom of the _____.

4. In a transverse wave, an object in the wave moves (side to side / up and down).

5. The movement of an object in longitudinal and transverse waves is   (the same /

   different).

Wave Frequency

Wave frequency is the number of waves that pass a point in a given unit of time. In the diagram below, A—B is a cycle. C—D is a cycle. Note that at "B" the wave starts to repeat its pattern. At the end of a cycle, the wave begins to repeat its pattern. Each cycle is completed in one period. A **period** is the time it takes to complete one cycle. A period may be one second or more. Do not confuse period with frequency. Frequency is measuring how often something happens. Period measures how much time it takes for something to happen. Periods are measured in time. Frequency is measured in **hertz** (Hz). A frequency of one cycle per second is defined as a frequency of one hertz.

Name: _____ Date: _____

Use the diagram below, and answer the following.

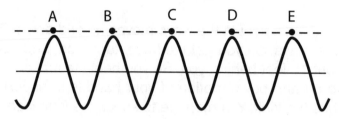

1. The cycle from "A" to "B" is from (trough to trough / crest to crest).

2. The letter "C" is the end of a cycle that began with letter

    a) A.   b) B.   c) C.   d) D.

3. The cycle from "C" to "D" is from (trough to trough / crest to crest).

4. The letter "E" is the end of a cycle that began with the letter

    a) C.   b) D.   c) E.   d) A.

5. It takes one-half second for A—B. The period for each cycle is _____ second.

6. Wave frequency for A—B is   a) 1   b) 2   c) 3   d) 4   per second.

Finding Wave Frequency

To find the frequency of a wave, remember that frequency is the number of cycles that occur in a given amount of time. So the formula to find wave frequency is **frequency = cycles ÷ second.** The unit we use to measure frequency is the Hertz (Hz). One Hz is equal to one cycle per second.

> **Example:** A wave makes 3 cycles per second.
> frequency = 3 cycles ÷ 1 second
> frequency = 3 ÷ 1
> frequency = 3 Hz.

1. It takes 2 seconds for a wave cycle.   f = cycles ÷ seconds   f = 1 ÷ _____

    frequency = _____ cycle each second

2. It takes 4 seconds for a wave cycle.   f = cycles ÷ seconds   f = 1 ÷ _____

    frequency = _____ cycle each second

3. A wave cycle is 6 seconds.   f = cycles ÷ seconds   f = 1 ÷ _____

    frequency = _____ cycles each second

4. The wave cycle is $\frac{1}{2}$ second. $f = 1 \div \frac{1}{2}$ $f = 1 \bullet \frac{2}{1}$ $f = 1 \bullet$ _____

    frequency = _____ cycles each second

Name: _____ Date: _____

Wavelength and Speed

Remember, **wavelength** is the distance from crest to crest or the distance from trough to trough. This a wave cycle. Frequency is the number of wave crests that pass a given point in a given unit of time. How can you determine the wavelength? The formula is **Wavelength = Speed ÷ Frequency**. Keep in mind that speed is different from frequency. Speed measures the distance a wave covers, in miles or meters, in a certain amount of time. Frequency measures the number of cycles per second. A wave can have a low frequency, 2 Hz, but still be moving quickly over a great distance. A wave can also have a high frequency, 376 Hz, but only have a speed of one centimeter per second.

Complete the following.

1. A wave is traveling at a speed of 4 meters per second. The frequency is 1 cycle per second. Wavelength = _____ m ÷ _____ Hz   Wavelength = _____ ÷ _____

    Wavelength = _____ m

2. A wave is traveling at a speed of 4 meters per second. The frequency is 2 cycles per second. Wavelength = _____ m ÷ _____ Hz   Wavelength = _____ ÷ _____

    Wavelength = _____ m

3. A wave is traveling at a speed of 8 meters per second. The frequency is 1 cycle per second. Wavelength = _____ m ÷ _____ Hz   Wavelength = _____ m

4. A wave is traveling at a speed of $\frac{1}{2}$ meter per second. The frequency is 2 cycles per second. Wavelength = _____ m ÷ _____ Hz   Wavelength = _____ m

5. A wave is traveling at a speed of 12 meters per second. The frequency is 6 cycles per second. Wavelength = _____ m ÷ _____ Hz Wavelength = _____ m

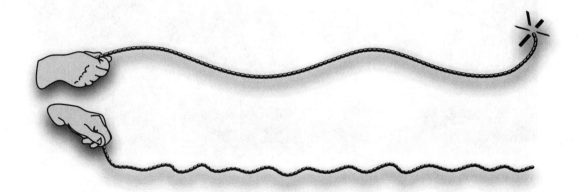

Name: _____ Date: _____

Wave Speed

To find the speed of a wave, we use the same formula we used to find the wavelength, but we rearrange it a bit. Instead of **Wavelength = Speed ÷ Frequency**, we multiply both sides by frequency to isolate speed on one side of the equation. So the formula for finding the speed of a wave is **Speed = Wavelength • Frequency**. Remember, speed is measured in miles or meters per hour or second.

Complete the following.

1. A wavelength is 4 meters. The wave frequency is 1 cycle per second.

    Speed = _____ m • _____ Hz   Speed = _____ meters per second

2. A wavelength is 4 meters. The frequency is 2 cycles per second.

    Speed = _____ m • _____ Hz   Speed = _____ meters per second

3. A wavelength is 8 meters. The wave frequency is 1 cycle per second.

    Speed = _____ m • _____ Hz   Speed = _____ meters per second

4. A wavelength is 2 meters. The wave frequency is 4 cycles per second.

    Speed = _____ m • _____ Hz   Speed = _____ meters per second

5. A wavelength is 12 meters. The frequency is 6 cycles per second.

    Speed = _____ m • _____ Hz   Speed = _____ meters per second

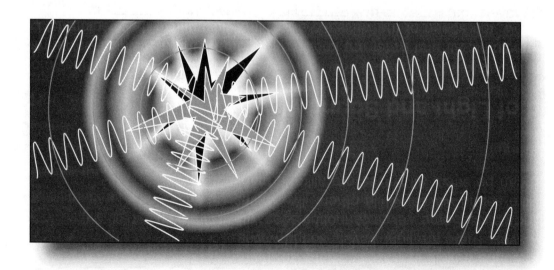

Name: _____ Date: _____

Chapter XII: Kepler's Laws

Johannes Kepler

In the early 1600s, a scientist named Johannes Kepler proposed three laws that explained the motion of the earth and other planets around the sun. These laws are still the best way of understanding how our solar system works. In this chapter, we will focus on the first two laws: the Law of Ellipses and the Law of Equal Areas.

The Law of Ellipses

Kepler's first law stated that the orbits of the planets around the sun are elliptical in shape, and that the sun is located at one of the focus points. What does that mean? As you can see in the diagram below, an **ellipse** is an oval shape with two foci, or focus points. The **foci** of an ellipse are on either side of the central axis of the ellipse. This is different from a circle. A circle has one focus. The focus in a circle is at the center of the circle.

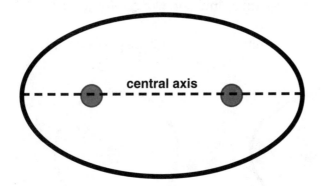

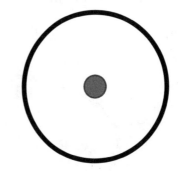

This diagram illustrates how to draw an ellipse. First, put two tacks into a piece of cardboard. Then tie a piece of string into a loop and wrap that loop around the two tacks. Next, take your pencil and use it to pull the string into a triangle shape. Slowly begin to trace out a path with the pencil, being sure to keep the string tight. When you have finished, you will have an elliptical shape. This is the shape of the orbit of Earth around the sun.

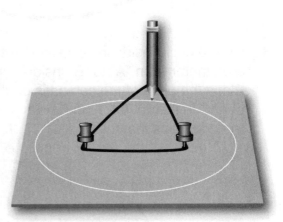

Name: _____ Date: _____

Answer the following.

1. Which object is an ellipse? Place the letter "E" on the blank if the object is shaped like an ellipse. Place the letter "C" on the blank if the object is shaped like a circle.

_____ a. An orange   _____ e. A baseball

_____ b. A football   _____ f. A jellybean

_____ c. A basketball   _____ g. A lemon

_____ d. An egg

Identifying the Major and Minor Axes

If the earth orbited in a circle, it would have the same axis at all times. That means that the earth would always be the same distance from the sun as it revolved around it. But the earth orbits the sun in an ellipse. An ellipse has 2 axes—a major axis and a minor axis. The major axis describes the line that passes through both foci points. The minor axis is the line that passes in between the two foci points. In a circle, both axes pass through the center focus.

2. In the diagram below, draw the major and minor axes in the ellipse and the axes in the circle.

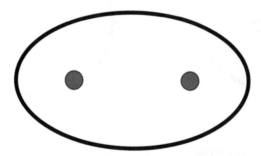 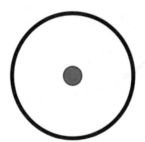

3. Draw a circle inside the ellipse. The ellipse below has a dot in the center. Draw a circle with a diameter from "A" to "B" inside the ellipse. You will need a compass to draw the circle. Place the point of the compass on the dot (C) and the other end of the compass with the pencil on the dot for "A" or "B" on the ellipse. Then, draw a circle inside the ellipse. Answer the questions that follow.

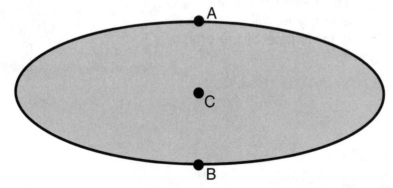

Name: _____ Date: _____

4. Read the statements below about the ellipse and circle in #3. Place a plus sign (+) on the blank before the true statements. Place a minus sign (–) on the blank if the statement is false.

Circumference of the ellipse = ⬭   Area of the ellipse = ⬬

Circumference of the circle = ◯   Area of the circle = ⬤

_____ a. The ellipse and circle have the same area.

_____ b. The area of the ellipse is larger than the area of the circle.

_____ c. The area of the circle is larger than the area of the ellipse.

_____ d. The circumference of the circle is greater than the circumference of the ellipse.

_____ e. The circumference of the ellipse is greater than the circumference of the circle.

_____ f. The circle has one focus.

_____ g. The ellipse has two foci.

5. *Comparing an ellipse and a circle*

Geometric Figure A below is an ellipse. Geometric Figure B on the next page is a circle.

Figure A

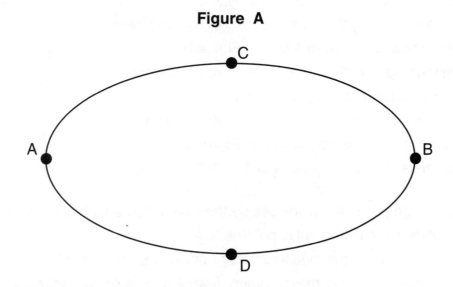

a. Draw a line from A to B and a line from C to D.

b. Write the term "major axis" along the line A to B.

c. Write the term "minor axis" along the line C to D.

d. The major axis and minor axis are (equal / unequal) in an ellipse.

109

Name: _____ Date: _____

Figure B

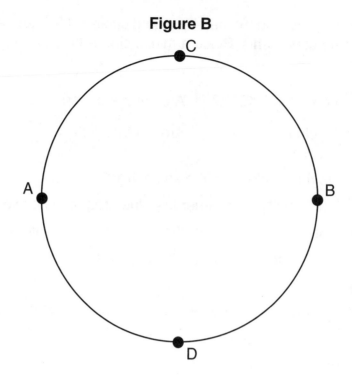

e. Draw a line from A to B and a line from C to D.

f. Write the term "axis" along the line A to B.

g. Write the term "axis" along the line C to D.

h. All the axes are (equal / unequal) in a circle.

i. Measure the distance from A to B in Figure A.

   The distance is   a) 2   b) 4   c) 5   d) 6   inches.

j. Measure the distance from A to B in Figure B.

   The distance is   a) 3   b) 5   c) 6   d) 7   inches.

k. Measure the distance from C to D in Figure A.

   The distance is   a) 1   b) 5   c) 6   d) 2   inches.

l. Measure the distance from C to D in Figure B.

   The distance is   a) 1   b) 3   c) 4   d) 5   inches.

6. Place a plus sign (+) on the blank beside the true statements below. Place a minus sign (–) on the blank if the statement is not true.

   _____ a. In the ellipse, the measurements from A to B and from C to D are the same.

   _____ b. In the ellipse, the measurement from A to B is greater than the measurement from C to D.

   _____ c. In the ellipse, the measurement from C to D is less than the measurement from A to B.

Name: _____ Date: _____

_____ d. In the circle, the measurement from A to B is greater than the measurement from C to D.

_____ e. In the circle, the measurement from C to D is greater than the measurement from A to B.

_____ f. In the circle, the measurements from A to B and from C to D are the same.

Earth's Elliptical Orbit

As we have already established, the earth moves in an elliptical orbit around the sun. The speeds at which the earth orbits are constantly changing. Because of the gravitational pull of the sun (which we learned about in Chapter IV), the speed of the earth increases as the earth gets closer to the sun. When the earth is closer to the sun, it is on the minor axis of the ellipse. When the earth is farther away from the sun, it is on the major axis of the ellipse. This is when the earth moves at its slowest. The length of the arrows on the diagram represent the speed of the earth as it revolves around the sun. The longer the arrow, the greater the speed.

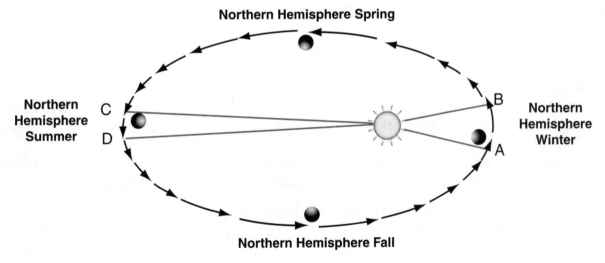

Use the diagram to answer the questions below.

1. The speed of the earth in its orbit is   a) faster   b) slower   during the Northern Hemisphere summer and winter.

2. The earth is farthest from the sun during the   a) Northern Hemisphere winter
    b) Northern Hemisphere summer.

As the earth travels around the sun, it takes the same amount of time to travel from A to B and from C to D. The travel time periods are equal, so the earth sweeps out equal areas of the ellipse. The sun and points A and B form a triangle. The sun and points C and D form a triangle.

Name: _____ Date: _____

    This is **Kepler's Second Law,** known as **the Law of Equal Areas.** This law says that the area of the triangle A to B is equal to the area of the triangle C to D.

3. The distance traveled along the orbit is greater in   a) A to B.   b) C to D.

4. The difference in distance traveled along the orbit is because the earth's speed is greater between   a) A and B.   b) C and D.

5. The earth sweeps out equal areas in orbit when

    a) the time periods in the orbit are the same.

    b) the speed of travel in the orbit periods are the same.

The Law of Equal Areas

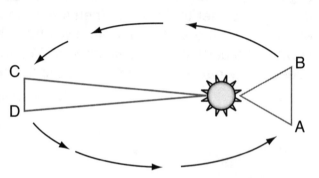

    Look at the diagram again. The sun and points A and B form a triangle. The sun and points C and D form a triangle. Kepler's Second Law describes the speed of a planet as it moves around the sun. It states that it takes the same amount of time for a planet to travel from A to B as it does for a planet to travel from C to D. The law also states that a planet will cover the same area in that time. In other words, as Earth moves around the sun, it always covers the same area in the same amount of time. The sides of the triangles may differ, but the areas of the triangles are the same.

    How can we figure out the area an object following an elliptical path covers? Remember the formula for a triangle. To find the area of a triangle, you multiply the height of a triangle by $\frac{1}{2}$ the base. The formula looks like this: area $= \frac{1}{2}$ base • height, or a $= \frac{1}{2}$ b • h.

    In comparing line A—B to line C—D, note that in line C—D, the earth's speed is slower, so the earth does not travel as far in its orbit. Therefore, the width (base) of the triangle is smaller. However, the earth is farther from the sun. So the height of the triangle is greater.

Solve the following.

    Area $= \frac{1}{2}$ base • height

1. The triangle below has a base of 6 inches and a height of 9 inches. Find the area.

    Area $= \frac{1}{2}$ • _____ inches • _____ inches. Area $= \frac{1}{2}$ • _____

    Area = _____ square inches

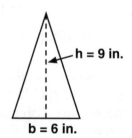

Name: _____ Date: _____

2. Triangle A below has a base of 2 inches and a height of 6 inches.

    Triangle B has a base of 4 inches and a height of 3 inches.

    Find the areas of Triangles A and B.

    a. Triangle A: Area = $\frac{1}{2}$ • _____ in. • _____ in.   Area = $\frac{1}{2}$ • _____ square inches

        Area = _____ square inches

    b. Triangle B: Area = $\frac{1}{2}$ • _____ in. • _____ in.   Area = $\frac{1}{2}$ • _____ square inches

        Area = _____ square inches

    c. Triangles A and B have   a) equal   b) unequal   areas.

Triangle A   **Triangle B**

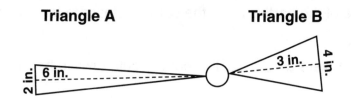

3. Triangle C below has a base of 1 inch and a height of 12 inches.

    Triangle D has a base of 2 inches and a height of 3 inches.

    Find the areas of Triangles C and D.

    a. Triangle C: Area = $\frac{1}{2}$ • _____ in. • _____ in.   Area = $\frac{1}{2}$ • _____ square inches

        Area = _____ square inches

    b. Triangle D: Area = $\frac{1}{2}$ • _____ in. • _____ in.   Area = $\frac{1}{2}$ • _____ square inches

        Area = _____ square inches

    c. Triangles C and D have   a) equal   b) unequal   areas.

Triangle C   **Triangle D**

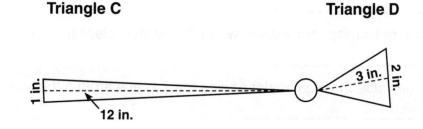

Name: _____ Date: _____

Reviewing Earth's Orbit

Use the numbers below to complete the blanks.

1. ellipse	2. elliptical	3. earth	4. Northern Hemisphere
5. orbit	6. circle	7. gravity	8. gravitational
9. winter	10. sun	11. space	12. planets

a. The path of the earth around the sun is called the earth's _____.

b. The shape of the orbit of the earth as it travels around the sun is not a circle, it is an _____.

c. The earth is kept from flying off into space by the pull of the sun's _____.

d. The orbit of the earth is shaped like an egg and is known as an _____ orbit.

e. Because of the elliptical shape of the earth's orbit, the earth is closer to the sun during the Northern Hemisphere _____.

f. If the shape of the earth's orbit were a _____, the earth would always be the same distance from the _____.

g. If it were not for the gravitational pull of the sun, the earth would fly off into _____.

h. The earth is one of the eight major _____ that revolves around the sun.

Read the clue and unscramble the following letters to make a word.

1. The path of the earth around the sun is not this figure.

   irclec ___ ___ ___ ___ ___ ___

2. This word describes the figure that is the path of the earth around the sun.

   lieples ___ ___ ___ ___ ___ ___ ___

3. This word describes the pull of the sun on the earth.

   ragivyt ___ ___ ___ ___ ___ ___ ___

4. The earth stays in this as it revolves around the sun.

   tbroi ___ ___ ___ ___ ___

5. This word is the Northern Hemisphere season when the earth is closest to the sun.

   rwient ___ ___ ___ ___ ___ ___

6. This word is used to describe the eight major bodies that revolve around the sun.

   snpleat ___ ___ ___ ___ ___ ___ ___

Answer Keys

Chapter I: Atoms, Molecules, and Compounds
Protons, Neutrons, and Electrons (page 4)

1. atom   2. protons, neutrons, electrons   3. proton
4. electrons   5. neutrons   6. equal   7. electrons
8. positive   9. negative

Elements (page 5)

1. 8   2. 79   3. 26   4. 2   5. 1

Molecules (page 5)

A. SE   B. SE   C. DE
1. oxygen   2. hydrogen, oxygen

Compounds (page 6)

1. E   2. C   3. C   4. C   5. E

Mixtures (page 6)

1. +   2. +   3. −   4. +   5. +   6. +   7. −   8. −

Chapter II: Chemistry
Periodic Table Symbols (page 7)

1. Au   2. He   3. Ne   4. Al   5. Ra   6. Cs   7. Cl   8. S

Atomic Number (page 8)

1. Al, 13   2. O, 8   3. Fe, 26   4. Pb, 82   5. Hg, 80   6. Na, 11
7. Cu, 29   8. Au, 79   9. He, 2   10. Ra, 88   11. Rn, 86   12. C, 6
13. Ni, 28   14. H, 1   15. K, 19   16. Ne, 10   17. N, 7   18. Zn, 30
19. Co, 27   20. P, 15   21. Ca, 20

Chemical Formulas (page 9)

1. 2: hydrogen, oxygen   2. 2: carbon, oxygen
3. 3: lead, sulfur, oxygen   4. 2: sodium, oxygen
5. hydrogen, oxygen   6. carbon, oxygen
7. lead, sulfur, oxygen   8. sodium, oxygen

Review (page 9)

1. D   2. E   3. A   4. B   5. C   6. F

Chapter III: States of Matter
Matter (page 10)

1. solids   2. liquids/gases   3. gases/liquids   4. atoms   5. liquids
6. solid   7. gases

Volume (page 11)

B. should be $\frac{1}{5}$ filled, C. $\frac{1}{2}$ filled, and D. $\frac{1}{8}$ filled. Teacher check that approximate liquid levels are shaded.

Density (page 12)

1. different   2. different   3. different   4. more   5. more   6. less
7. atoms

Boyle's Law for Gas (page 13)

1. a   2. b   3. d   4. unchanged   5. decreases

Chapter IV: Mass, Weight, Gravity, and Density
Matter, Mass, and Weight (page 14)

1. F   2. F   3. T   4. T   5. T
6. F   7. T   8. T   9. F   10. T

Mass Measurement (page 15)

	Grams	Kilograms	Pounds
1.	500	0.5	1.1
2.	2,000	2	4.4
3.	4,000	4	8.8
4.	4,500	4.5	9.9
5.	5,000	5	11
6.	7,000	7	15.4
7.	10,000	10	22
8.	1,500	1.5	3.3
9.	100	0.1	0.22
10.	250	0.25	0.55

Weight on Earth (pages 16–17)

1. d   2. b   3. c   4. d   5. b
6. T   7. T   8. T   9. F   10. T   11. F   12. T

Weight and Gravity on Earth and the Moon (page 17)

1. c   2. b   3. a   4. a

Converting Pounds to Newtons (page 18)

1. 4.5   2. 45   3. 450   4. 675   5. 900

Converting Newtons to Pounds (page 18)

6. 2.25   7. 30   8. 175   9. 80   10. 500

Converting Kilograms to Newtons (page 18)

11. 9.8   12. 98   13. 980   14. 4,900   15. 9,800

Converting Newtons to Kilograms (page 18)

16. 1   17. 10   18. 100   19. 1,010   20. 101,010

Newton's Law of Gravity (page 20)

1. $Fg = (1,000 \cdot 40) / 30^2$ $Fg = 44.4$
3. increased, decreased
2. $Fg = (1,000 \cdot 40) / 60^2$ $Fg = 11.1$
4. $Fg = (1,000 \cdot 40) / 90^2$ $Fg = 4.9$

Newtons and Force (page 21)

1. $F = (1 \text{ kg} \cdot 1 \text{ m}) / 1 \text{ s}^2$ $F = 1 \text{ N}$
2. $F = (3 \text{ kg} \cdot 1 \text{ m}) / 1 \text{ s}^2$ $F = 3 \text{ N}$
3. $F = (5 \text{ kg} \cdot 1 \text{ m}) / 1 \text{ s}^2$ $F = 5 \text{ N}$
4. $F = (10 \text{ kg} \cdot 1 \text{ m}) / 1 \text{ s}^2$ $F = 10 \text{ N}$
5. $F = (100 \text{ kg} \cdot 1 \text{ m}) / 1 \text{ s}^2$ $F = 100 \text{ N}$
6. $F = (10 \text{ kg} \cdot 1 \text{ m}) / 2 \text{ s}^2$ $F = (10 \cdot 1) / 4$ $F = 10 / 4$ $F = 2.5 \text{ N}$

Dynes (page 22)

1. 980   2. 1,960   3. 2,940   4. 4,900   5. 9,800
6. 49,000   7. 98,000   8. 980,000

More Volume and Density
Volume of Rectangular Prisms and Cubes (page 23)

1. b   2. c   3. a

Volume: Matching (page 24)

1. D   2. E   3. C   4. B   5. A

Find the Volume: Rectangles and Squares (page 24)

1. Volume = $10 \cdot 5 \cdot 3$; Volume = 150 cubic inches
2. Volume = $5 \cdot 4 \cdot 1$; Volume = 20 cubic feet
3. Volume = $8 \cdot 4 \cdot 2$; Volume = 64 cubic yards
4. Volume = $5 \cdot 2 \cdot 1$; Volume = 10 cm³
5. Volume = $20 \cdot 4 \cdot 2$; Volume = 160 cm³
6. Volume = $3 \cdot 2 \cdot 2$; Volume = 12 m³
7. Volume = $4 \cdot 3 \cdot 4$; Volume = 48 cubic c) yards
8. Volume = $5 \cdot 6 \cdot 3$; Volume = 90 cubic feet
   60 in. length, 72 in. width, 36 in. height
   Volume in inches c) 155,520
9. Volume = $2 \cdot 2 \cdot 1$; Volume = 4 cubic meters
   200 cm length, 200 cm width, 100 cm height
   Volume = $200 \cdot 200 \cdot 100$; Volume = 4,000,000 cm³

Volume of Spheres (page 25)

1.–3. Teacher check that diagram is labeled correctly.
4. 8   5. 27   6. 64   7. $5 \cdot 5 \cdot 5 = 125$
8. 6^3; $6 \cdot 6 \cdot 6 = 216$ 9. 8; 25.12; 25   10. 27; 84.78; 85
11. 64; 200.96; 201   12. 125; 392.5; 393   13. 512; 1,607.68; 1,608

Find the Volume for These Spheres (page 26)

1. Step 1: $3^3 = 3 \cdot 3 \cdot 3$ Step 2: $84.78 = 85$ Step 3: $\frac{85}{1} = \frac{340}{3} = 113.33$

2. Step 1: $4^3 = 4 \cdot 4 \cdot 4$ Step 2: $200.96 = 201$ Step 3: $\frac{201}{1} = \frac{804}{3} = 268$

3. Step 1: $5^3 = 5 \cdot 5 \cdot 5$ Step 2: $125 = 392.5 = 393$ Step 3: $\frac{393}{1} = \frac{1572}{3} = 524$

Density (page 27)

1. $D = 38.6 \text{ g} \div 2 \text{ cm}^3$
2. $D = 23.4 \text{ g} \div 3 \text{ cm}^3$
3. $D = 9 \text{ g} \div 9 \text{ cm}^3$ $D = 1 \text{ g/cm}^3$
4. $D = 10.8 \text{ g} \div 2 \text{ cm}^3$ $D = 5.4 \text{ g/cm}^3$
5. $D = 24 \text{ g} \div 4 \text{ cm}^3$ $D = 6 \text{ g/cm}^3$

Buoyancy (page 28)

Density of water: 1 g/cm^3 Density of cork: 0.25 g/cm^3 Density of iron: 7.8 g/cm^3

1. $3 \text{ g} / 3 \text{ cm}^3$; 1 g/cm^3
2. $1 \text{ g} / 4 \text{ cm}^3$; 0.25; 0.25 g/cm^3
3. $31.5 \text{ g} / 4 \text{ cm}^3 = 31.5 \div 4 = 7.8$ $D = 7.8 \text{ g/cm}^3$
4. greater, float   5. greater, sink

Displacement: Float or Sink? (page 29)

1. F   2. S   3. F   4. S   5. S
6. a   7. b   8. a   9. b   10. 5 oz.; c

Density of Steel and Water (page 30)

1. $W = 40 \cdot 488$ $W = 19,520$ pounds   2. $W = 40 \cdot 62.4$ $W = 2,496$ pounds
3. b   4. 19,520

Buoyancy and Ships (pages 30–31)

1. b   2. a   3. a   4. b   5. b   6. 1,952   7. a   8. a

Chapter V: Newton's Laws of Motion
Newton's First Law of Motion (page 32)

a. 4   b. 3   c. 2   d. 1

Newton's Second Law of Motion (page 33)

1. T   2. F   3. F   4. T   5. T

Speed and Velocity (page 34)

1. S   2. V   3. S   4. V   5. V

Acceleration: True or False (page 34)

1. F   2. F   3. T   4. T   5. T   6. F   7. T   8. T

Acceleration: Solve (page 35)
1. 1 newton, 1 kilogram, 1 meter per second
2. 2 newtons, 1 kilogram, 1 kg, 2 meters per second
3. 8 newtons, 1 kilogram, 1 kg, 8 meters per second
4. 10 newtons, 1 kilogram, 10 N, 10 meters per second
5. force, newtons, mass, kilogram, 12, 12 meters per second
6. 0.5   7. 4, 0.25   8. 2, 2 ÷ 1, 4   9. 5, 2   10. 12, 3
11. decreases   12. increases

Acceleration: Matching (page 36)
1. E   2. C   3. B   4. F   5. A   6. G   7. D

Speed and Distance of Falling Objects (pages 36–37)
1. 4.9   2. 14.7   3. 24.5   4. 34.3   5. 44.1
6. 4.9   7. 14.7   8. 24.5   9. 34.3   10. 44.1
11. 9.8   12. See graph below.   13. 9.8

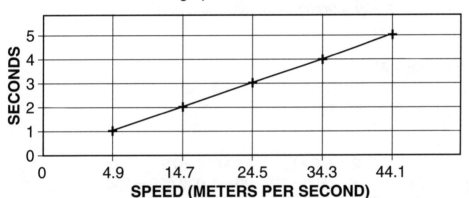

Distance Object Falls (page 37)
1. $1 \cdot 1 = 1$ 2. $2 \cdot 2 = 4$ 3. $3 \cdot 3 = 9$ 4. $4 \cdot 4 = 16$
5. $5 \cdot 5 = 25$ 6. $6 \cdot 6 = 36$ 7. $7 \cdot 7 = 49$ 8. 64
9. 81   10. 100

Distance Chart (page 38)
1. 1   2. 2, 19.6   3. 4.9, 3, 9, 44.1   4. 4.9, 4, 78.4
5. $d = 4.9t^2$, $d = 4.9 \cdot 5^2$, $d = 4.9 \cdot 25$, 122.5 m
6. See graph below.   7. b

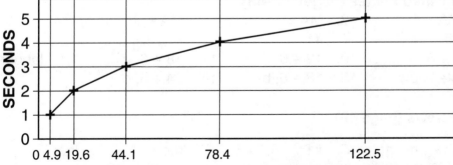

119

Newton's Third Law of Motion (page 39)
1. T   2. T   3. T   4. F   5. F

Chapter VI: Simple Machines
The Meaning of Work (page 40)
1. W, both are +   2. W, both are +   3. NW, both are –
4. NW, + A force was applied., – Work was done.

Using the English System to Measure Work (page 41)
1. a   2. b   3. a   4. +   5. +   6. –   7. +   8. –
9. W = 30 • 10, W = 300   10. W = 60 • 4, W = 240   11. W = 100 • 5, W = 500
12. W = 300 • 10, W = 3,000   13. W = 1,000 • 20, W = 20,000

Using the Metric System to Measure Work (page 42)
1. a   2. b   3. c
4. W = 20 • 10, W = 200   5. W = 50 • 3, W = 150
6. W = 400 • 4, W = 1,600   7. W = 20,000 • 20, W = 400,000
8. W = 200 • 2, W = 400

Equivalent Amounts of Work (page 43)
1. a) 4   b) 2   2. a) 3   b) 2   3. a) 300 b) 12
4. a) 4   b) 400   5. a) 250 b) 3

Power (pages 43–44)
1. 400 / 2 = 200   2. (60 • 5) / 4 = 300 / 4 = 75
3. (100 • 10) / 5 = 1,000 / 5 = 200   4. (500 • 10) / 20 = 5,000 / 20 = 250
5. (1,600 • 10) / 40 = 16,000 / 40 = 400

Mechanical Advantage (page 45)
1. MA = 4   2. MA = 5   3. MA = 3   4. MA = 4   5. MA = 11
6. #5   7. #1

Mechanical Advantage: Levers (page 46)
1. 4 to 2, MA = 2   2. 12 to 4, MA = 3   3. 5 to 1, MA = 5
4. 15 to 5, MA = 3   5. 6 to 3, MA = 2   6. #3   7. #1 and #5

Mechanical Advantage: Inclined Planes (pages 47–48)
1. MA = 3   2. MA = 4   3. MA = 5   4. MA = 6
5. MA = 10   6. #5   7. #1
8. 7 ÷ 6, a   9. 8 ÷ 6, b   10. 12 ÷ 6, d   11. 18 ÷ 6, c   12. longer
13. 6 ÷ 2, d   14. 8 ÷ 4, c   15. 18 ÷ 6, b   16. 24 ÷ 3, c

Mechanical Advantage: Screws (page 49)
1. $\frac{1}{8}$ 2. $\frac{1}{10}$ 3. $\frac{1}{4}$ 4. $\frac{1}{16}$ 5. #1   6. #3   7. more   8. less

Mechanical Advantage: Wedges (page 50)
1. MA = 2   2. MA = 4   3. MA = 2   4. MA = 4   5. MA = 10
6. #5   7. #1 and #3

Mechanical Advantage: Wheel and Axle (pages 51–52)
1. 40 to 10, 4 to 1, MA = 4, 4   2. 10 to 2, 5 to 1, MA = 5, 5
3. 36 to 3, 12 to 1, MA = 12, 12

Gears (pages 52–53)
1. b   2. c   3. c   4. d   5. b   6. a   7. c   8. b

Gear Ratio (page 53)
1. b   2. a   3. b   4. c   5. a   6. d   7. c   8. a

Torque (page 54)
1. d   2. b   3. a   4. c   5. a   6. a   7. a   8. b
9. b   10. c

Mechanical Advantage: Pulleys (page 56)
1. 2   2. a   3. b   4. 4   5. c   6. a   7. d   8. b

Chapter VII: Vectors
Scalar and Vector Measurements (page 57)
1. S   2. S   3. V   4. V   5. S   6. S
7. V   8. S   9. S   10. V

Magnitude and Direction of Vectors (pages 58–59)
1. c   2. b   3. d   4. b   5. a, f   6. d, g   7. c, e
8. c, h   9. b, g

The Coordinate System (pages 59–60)
1. c   2. a   3. c   4. b   5. c

Displacement (pages 61–63)
1. + no displacement   2. + displacement
3. a   4. a   5. a   6. a   7. b   8. a

Speed or Velocity? (page 64)
1. + speed only   2. + speed only   3. + speed and direction
4. + speed and direction   5. + speed only

Acceleration (page 65)
1. V   2. V   3. A   4. A

Average Rate of Acceleration (pages 65–66)
1. 1   2. 50   3. 5   4. 0.025   5. 0.5

Acceleration Vectors and Direction (page 67)
1. d   2. d   3. a   4. a

Chapter VIII: Static Electricity
Electrical Charge in Atoms: Bohr Model of the Atom (page 68)
1. Teacher check that diagram is labeled correctly.
   a. nucleus   b. protons   c. neutrons   d. electrons

Electrical Charge in Atoms: Glass and Rubber Rods (pages 69–70)
2. Glass rod +; Rubber rod –   3. A   4. C   5. B   6. a   7. b   8. a

Electrical Charge in Atoms: Static Electricity (page 70)
9., 10., 12., and 13. +

Grounding (page 71)
1. NG   2. G   3. G   4. NG   5. G

Humidity and Static Electricity (page 72)
1. and 5. +   6. increase   7. increase   8. frequently   9. quickly   10. winter

Lightning (page 73)
1. b   2. a   3. b
4. Teacher check cloud diagrams. Lightning arrows should go from – signs in one cloud to + signs in another cloud.

Lightning Rods (page 74)
1. F   2. T   3. T   4. T   5. F

Static Electricity Review (pages 74–75)
1. positive   2. negative   3. protons   4. electrons   5. repel   6. attracts
7. attracts   8. repel
9. Teacher check diagram. Lightning arrows should go from – signs in bottom of cloud to the + signs in the lone tree and the church steeple. Responses should include that the lone tree and church steeple have a positive charge, so lightning will go from the negative cloud bottom to the positive charge.

Chapter IX: Electricity
Watts (page 77)
1. W = 50 • 2; W = 100   2. W = 40 • 1.5; W = 60
3. W = 120 • 5; W = 600   4. W = 120 • 8; W = 960

Kilowatts (page 77)
1. W = 120 • 15; W = 1,800; KW = 1.8
2. W = 120 • 22; W = 2,640; KW = 2.64
3. W = 120 • 33; W = 3,960; KW = 3.96
4. W = 120 • 45; W = 5,400; KW = 5.4

Watt-hours (page 78)
1. 100 W • 2 hrs. = 200 watt-hours
2. 40 W • 4 hrs. = 160 watt-hours
3. 75 W • 10 hrs. = 750 watt-hours
4. 100 W • 10 hrs. = 1,000 watt-hours

Kilowatt-hours (pages 78–79)
1. c   2. b   3. a   4. d   5. d   6. b   7. a   8. c
9. $390   10. $11.70   11. $1.50   12. $0.72

Resistance (pages 80–81)
1. a   2. a   3. b   4. A   5. B

Ohm's Law (page 81)
1. $R\Omega = 1.5 / 0.3$; $R\Omega = 5$
2. $R\Omega = 3/ 0.3$; $R\Omega = 10$
3. $R\Omega = 6 / 2$; $R\Omega = 3$
4. $R\Omega = 12 / 2$; $R\Omega = 6$

Amperes (page 82)
1. I = 6 / 30; I = 0.2 amperes
2. I = 3 / 15; I = 0.2 amperes
3. I = 12 / 24; I = 0.5 amperes
4. I = 4.5 / 15; I = 0.3 amperes

Voltage (page 82)
1. V = 0.2 • 30; V = 6
2. V = 2 • 2; V = 4
3. V = 30 • 4; V = 120
4. V = 0.5 • 3; V = 1.5

Circuits (page 83)
1. Teacher check that diagram is labeled correctly.
   A. light bulb, B. filament, C. positive battery post, D. negative battery post, E. wire
2. resists   3. the battery   4. negative

Lights Wired in Series (page 84)
Teacher check that diagram is labeled correctly.
A. + positive post, B. – negative post, C. copper wire, D. light bulb, E. filament
1. b   2. b   3. a   4. one   5. increases

Lights Wired in Parallel (page 85)
Teacher check that diagram is labeled correctly.
A. flow of electrons, B. lightbulbs, C. battery, D. copper wire
1. a   2. a   3. a   4. a   5. b   6. b

Switches (page 86)
1. C   2. O   3. C   4. O   5. O

Chapter X: Light Refraction and Reflection
Using the Protractor to Measure Angles of Incidence (page 88)
1. 30   2. 60   3. Teacher check. 4. c   5. Teacher check.   6. b

Determining the Angle of Reflection (page 89)
1. Teacher check.   2. b

Measuring the Angle of Reflection (pages 89–90)
1. Teacher check diagram. Angles are 60 degrees.
2. Teacher check diagram. Angles are 70 degrees.
3. Teacher check diagram. Angles are 50 degrees.
4. d   5. d   6. equal

Refracted Light Rays (page 91)
1. more dense   2. refracted   3. away from   4. arrow R
5. less dense   6. away from   7. arrow R   8. away from normal
9. away from normal

Complete the Diagram (page 92)
Teacher check diagram.

Learning About the Prism and Refracted Light (page 93)
Teacher check prism diagram.

Refracted and Reflected Light and Rainbows (page 94)
Teacher check water droplet diagram.
4. refracted   5. reflected

Wavelengths of Light (pages 94–95)
1. c   2. b   3. wavelength   4. wavelength, frequency
5. Teacher check rainbow diagram.

Identifying Terms Related to Rainbows and Prisms (page 95)
1. R   2. R   3. RP   4. RP   5. R   6. RP   7. RP   8. P

How Does the Human Eye See Color? (page 96)
Teacher check the human eye diagram.
a. lens, b. pupil, c. iris, d. cornea, e. retina, f. rods and cones, g. optic nerve

How Does the Human Eye See Color?: Select the Correct Answer (page 97)
1. b   2. d   3. a

Complete the Paragraphs (page 98)
      Normally, we see white light as it passes through air. However, each ray of white light
is made __2__. When a ray of white light enters a prism, the white light is slowed down. __1__ and
enters the prism causes the white light to __4__. When the refracted white light leaves a prism,

we can see the beautiful red, orange, yellow, green, blue, indigo, and violet colors. In the sky, the small spherical droplets of water _5_ . Rainbows develop because as the ray of white light enters the spherical droplet, the speed of the white light is slowed down and refracted.

   Light comes from the sun as _9_ . Rainbows are possible when the parallel rays of sunlight enter droplets of water in the atmosphere. The shape of the droplets of _7_ . When the sunlight enters the spherical droplet of water, the ray of light is _8_ . The ray of light then hits the inside wall of the droplet of water, and it is bounced, or reflected, to another part of the droplet. Then the ray of light departs, or leaves, the spherical droplet and is again bent. Imagine this happening in a sky that has many small _6_ . The droplets are all receiving light rays from the sun. The light rays are bent, _10_ , as they enter the droplets, then the light rays bounce, or are reflected. Finally the light rays depart from the droplets and are refracted again. The colors of the rainbow are then visible.

Chapter XI: Understanding Waves
Speed of Sound Waves (page 100)
1. a 2. more than 3. b 4. 2,000

Speed of Light Waves (page 100)
1. d 2. a

Understanding How Waves Are Alike (page 101)
1. Teacher check Diagram A.
2. Teacher check Diagram B.

Longitudinal Waves (page 102)
1. crest 2. trough 3. crest, trough 4. side to side

Transverse Waves (page 103)
1. crest 2. trough 3. crest, trough 4. up and down 5. different

Wave Frequency (page 104)
1. crest to crest 2. b 3. crest to crest 4. b 5. one-half 6. b

Finding Wave Frequency (page 104)
1. $f = 1 \div 2; f = \frac{1}{2}$ cycle each second 2. $f = 1 \div 4; f = \frac{1}{4}$ cycle each second
3. $f = 1 \div 6; f = \frac{1}{6}$ cycle each second 4. $f = 1 \bullet 2; f = 2$ cycles each second

Wavelength and Speed (page 105)
1. Wavelength = 4 m ÷ 1 Hz; Wavelength = 4 ÷ 1; Wavelength = 4 m
2. Wavelength = 4 m ÷ 2 Hz; Wavelength = 4 ÷ 2; Wavelength = 2 m
3. Wavelength = 8 m ÷ 1 Hz; Wavelength = 8 ÷ 1; Wavelength = 8 m
4. Wavelength = $\frac{1}{2}$ m ÷ 2 Hz; Wavelength = $\frac{1}{2} \div 2$; Wavelength = $\frac{1}{8}$ m
5. Wavelength = 12 m ÷ 6 Hz; Wavelength = 12 ÷ 6; Wavelength = 2 m

Wave Speed (page 106)
1. Speed = 4 m • 1 Hz; Speed = 4 meters per second
2. Speed = 4 m • 2 Hz; Speed = 8 meters per second
3. Speed = 8 m • 1 Hz; Speed = 8 meters per second
4. Speed = 2 m • 4 Hz; Speed = 8 meters per second
5. Speed = 12 m • 6 Hz; Speed = 72 meters per second

Chapter XII: Kepler's Laws
The Law of Ellipses (pages 108–111)
1. a. C   b. E   c. C   d. E   e. C   f. E   g. E
2. Teacher check diagrams.
3. Teacher check diagram.
4. a. –   b. +   c. –   d. –   e. +   f. +   g. +
5. Teacher check diagram for a., b., and c.   d. unequal
   e., f., and g. Teacher check diagram.   h. equal
   i. b   j. a   k. d   l. b
6. a. –   b. +   c. +   d. –   e. –   f. +

Earth's Elliptical Orbit (pages 111–112)
1. b   2. b   3. a   4. a   5. a

The Law of Equal Areas (pages 112–113)
1. Area = $\frac{1}{2}$ • 6 • 9; Area = $\frac{1}{2}$ • 54; Area = 27 square inches
2. a.   Area = $\frac{1}{2}$ • 2 • 6; Area = $\frac{1}{2}$ • 12; Area = 6 square inches
   b.   Area = $\frac{1}{2}$ • 4 • 3; Area = $\frac{1}{2}$ • 12; Area = 6 square inches
   c.   a
3. a.   Area = $\frac{1}{2}$ • 1 • 12; Area = $\frac{1}{2}$ • 12; Area = 6 square inches
   b.   Area = $\frac{1}{2}$ • 2 • 3; Area = $\frac{1}{2}$ • 6; Area = 3 square inches
   c.   b

Reviewing Earth's Orbit (page 114)
a. 5   b. 1   c. 7   d. 2   e. 9   f. 6, 10   g. 11   h. 12
1. circle   2. ellipse   3. gravity   4. orbit
5. winter   6. planets